Chinese Flower Painting Techniques

Stephen Cassettari

STUDIO VISTA

an imprint of
Cassell plc
Villiers House, 41/47 Strand
London WC2N 5JE

First published in United Kingdom 1992
by arrangement with Collins/Angus & Robertson Publishers Pty Limited, Sydney, Australia.

First published in Australia in 1992 by
Collins/Angus & Robertson.

British Library Cataloguing in Publication data

A catalogue record for Chinese Flower Painting Techniques *is available from the British Library.*

ISBN 0 289 80077 3

Printed in Hong Kong

5 4 3 2 1
96 95 94 93 92

CONTENTS

Dedicated to Amy Huang—
teacher and friend.

CHAPTER 1

INTRODUCTION

This book presents various techniques and subjects used in traditional Chinese flower painting. This category also includes birds, insects, fish and bamboo, as well as such natural elements as rocks and water, used for their complementary balancing effects.

Other classifications in Chinese painting are landscape, animals (including the larger birds), people, religious subjects and bamboo, which also appears in the other categories. The exclusive portrayal of bamboo can be a life-time study. Chinese Calligraphy is also included, being considered a variation of painting, even supreme to it.

There are two main styles from which other variations are derived:

BRUSH STYLE (Mo-Ku)—'Without bone'. The usual style for flowers, animals and bamboo.

This style emphasises use of the brush, with its ability to expressively produce strokes of varied thickness, combining multiple tones or colours within one movement. It transmits the 'Chi' life-spirit of the subject.

OUTLINE STYLE (Pa-Ku)—'With bone'. The usual style for landscape and people.

For this style the same brush is used in a more restrained and refined manner. It delineates the form of the subject in a variety of lines of different tone and quality, to convey the particular character of each element of the subject. A soft wash of colour is usually applied to enhance these characteristics.

Thus a flower will have a light, soft outline with a pale, translucent wash of pure colour to indicate its fragility, while a branch will have a dark, dry outline with an opaque wash in deep tones to indicate its strength.

The two styles can be combined in a variety of ways for degrees of interpretation, but always grace and harmony are maintained.

The variation of styles presented ranges from the elegantly classical to the relatively recent, more exuberant style, so that the techniques can be acquired to make an interpretation as individual as handwriting: a heart-print.

When all the techniques have been practised, understood and intuitively felt by being absorbed into the heart, then there will be an ability that can be applied when respectfully approaching nature (the ultimate teacher) for guidance and inspiration.

The heart is full of joy

ready to burst into song.

Words learnt long ago

are released to soar to the heavens.

Chinese brush painting is a visual language well suited to convey the universal images of flowers, the quintessence of the beauty of nature.

CHAPTER 2

THE HARMONY OF OPPOSITES

相对调和

The fundamental principle of Chinese philosophy, which is applied to all aspects of life including religion and art, is that everything that exists has a complementary and harmonious opposite, and that together these two become as one. That one is far greater than the sum of the separate parts. A very clear example of this would be when male and female together produce children to form a family, and many families make a nation. Thus from small things comes the whole, which also contains additional aspects.

In painting, this principle of harmonious opposites applies to the materials, the techniques, the subjects and to the spirit (inspiration) that guides the artist.

The soft, flexible, absorbent hairs of the brush are balanced by the rigid, strong bamboo handle. It allows for firm control in the dexterity of line and tone. This brush is placed in contact with the paper, which is soft and absorbent, but laid flat on a firm surface. It is the brush that gives and the paper that receives.

Within this technique the opposites are often referred to as the 'six principles' consisting of: fast and slow movement, thick and thin lines, the flower and the bird (subject), the painted areas and the empty spaces of paper (composition), light and dark tone, and old and new approaches of traditional interpretations of subjects.

An important concept of interpretation in Chinese painting is that each element of a subject is treated equally, thus the leaves and branches of a flower are portrayed as clearly as the petals.

The most important element is the artist, who uses the techniques to manipulate the materials to transform the subject into a painting, which is an object with a life of itself: it is within the artist that there is a meeting of heaven and earth, the energy source of mind and body.

That which is essential is not seen by the eye

but rather it is felt by the heart.

CHAPTER 3

THE FOUR TREASURES

If you are conversant with the equipment proceed to Chapter 4 to begin the exercises.

The basic equipment used in traditional Chinese painting is handmade from natural materials. It is precious both for the work that has gone into making it and because it is the means by which artists execute their craft.

BRUSH

The brush is usually made from animal hair set into a hollow bamboo handle. The better quality brushes have some sort of binding, or sometimes a piece of copper, where the handle joins the hair, to hold both together and prevent the bamboo from splitting. A piece of tape can be applied for the same purpose. There is usually a loop on the end of the handle so that the brush can be hung up to dry.

When you are starting off, you need just three brushes. A soft, white-haired brush made of goat's hair is a good brush to begin with, as it is easy to use, pliable and holds a lot of water. This type of brush is particularly suited to painting flower petals. You will also need a firmer, red-haired brush made of deer, squirrel or other animal hair, for painting leaves and for sharp line work. Also useful is a smaller vein brush made of similar hair for outline and fine detail work. Brushes are not numbered by size as are other painting brushes, but a wide variety of brushes designed for different uses are available.

CARE OF BRUSHES

After buying your brushes, discard the bamboo covers and soften the hairs in cold water. Always wash brushes in cold water and occasionally soap, never in hot water, and shape the brush tip to a point to dry. Carry your brushes in a rolled mat to protect the hairs.

INK-STICK

To begin with, a tube of black watercolour of student quality is good enough. It is better not to use acrylic or poster paint, and Indian or similar ink should definitely not be used, as these can destroy the hairs of the brush. Later you will need an ink-stick, which is made of solidified soot (usually pine) and fish glue. Don't buy the similar ink that is available in bottles, as this is designed for calligraphy and does not dilute well to produce the varying tones.

INK-STONE

You will also need an ink-stone to grind the ink. A simple ink-stone, either round with a lid or oblong with a shallow end, is best. The heavier, more expensive ones are made of natural stone.

To grind the ink, first place a cloth underneath the stone to prevent it from sliding. Wet the surface with just a couple of drops of water, hold the stick upright (as you would a brush) and grind it gently on the stone in a continuous motion, either up and down or round and round, until the ink is very dark (at least 5 to 10 minutes), adding more water as needed. The ink can be picked up with a brush directly from the stone or placed on a palette and mixed with water to achieve various tones of grey. Ink can be left for an hour or so if it is covered.

Don't leave the ink-stick standing on the stone, and don't hold the stick too tightly, as this could break the stick. Wash the ink-stone clean after each use.

PAPER

Newsprint, the paper newspapers are printed on, is the best paper to begin with. It can be bought in the form of scrap-books, or ends of rolls or blocks can be bought directly from a printer. Cartridge paper and most art papers are not suitable, as they are not absorbent enough.

After a little practice, it is advisable to begin using rice paper. This comes in rolls and sheets and is made from a variety of natural materials such as cotton, rice plant and mulberry. A very white paper made from cotton fibres is best for all-purpose work. Use the smooth side for most subjects—flowers, birds, people and so on—and the rough side for landscapes. Most rice paper is highly absorbent. Experiment with different types to discover which you like best for various effects. The finer the paper, the more control you have over the line; for example, a very fine, white paper is best for rendering the sharp strokes of pine, or for the outline style, and a very absorbent paper is best for soft flower petals.

Always carry rice paper rolled or in flat sheets. Never fold or crinkle it, as this makes the surface difficult to paint on. A cardboard tube is useful for carrying paper.

To tear rice paper, simply run a wet brush across the surface, making an even, thin line of water, and pull the paper apart slowly.

Once you have gained some practice on newsprint, the sooner you start using rice paper the better. You will get better results, and you will also learn the importance of working quickly. When using rice paper, first place a piece of newsprint or felt underneath to absorb any excess water that soaks through the paper.

OTHER EQUIPMENT

- Two small containers, one for washing the brush and one to hold clean water (which is essential when you are trying to achieve pure colours for flowers).
- A palette, or several small white saucers, or a white tray, for mixing colours and tones of black. (White is best, as it shows up the true colours.)
- An absorbent cotton cloth for soaking up excess water from the brush.
- A set of Chinese colours in tubes. Tubes are the most convenient form of colours. Originally the colours were also made in stick form, like the black ink-stick, from various

mineral and vegetable dyes. These can still be obtained; being softer than the black, they can be mixed on a small white saucer and do not require an ink-stone. They produce a paler colour, more suitable for washes, especially in landscape painting.

The colours can also be bought in pans. This form is best for painting flowers, because the consistency is thicker. Colour flakes are also available, but these are not as convenient and are not recommended.

All this equipment is obtainable from most well-stocked art suppliers. Most of it can be found in some Chinese or Japanese bookshops or even in oriental grocery shops, as this is the standard equipment used by children learning calligraphy.

The range of Chinese watercolours is different from that in a set of Western watercolours. The latter can be used, but you will need to mix them to obtain colours similar to the Chinese colours.

If you wish to use ordinary watercolours, you can buy them in individual tubes, for example from Windsor and Newton's Cotman range. The colours closest to the Chinese colours (and used in this book) are listed here (and will need to be mixed as explained in the instructions for individual paintings):

Red – Alizarin Crimson (for deep red)
– Rose Madder (for pink)
Blue – Indigo (for deep blue)
– Cerulean (for light blue)
Brown – Burnt Sienna
Yellow – Gamboge
Green – Traditionally mixed with gamboge and indigo, but sap green can also be used.
White – Used mainly for flowers and birds painted on coloured paper or silk.

Only water (not white) is used to lighten tones.

CHAPTER 4

PRACTICAL TECHNIQUES

PETALS, LEAVES, STEMS AND BRANCHES

This is a chapter of practise exercises to help you become familiar with the various brush strokes and methods of colour loading used to construct the compositions shown in later chapters.

BRUSH STROKES

The brush strokes are common to Chinese calligraphy as well as to all the other categories of Chinese painting. The double colour loading of the brush produces a two-toned effect, which gives added life and vitality to the brush strokes through the balance of the opposites of light and dark. The line of each brush stroke contains the balanced opposites of thick and thin.

Each stroke must have both of these qualities, a varied thick and thin line and a light and dark colour or tone, to be representative of the art of traditional Chinese painting.

BRUSHES

Red-Brown Brush (deer hair)—*resilient*—Holds its tip in shape well and therefore is most suitable to produce strokes with a pointed finish, such as sharp tipped leaves or thin petals: **needle and orchid strokes**.

Because this brush holds a fine point it is also suitable for fine control of the thickness of the line, such as for stems and vines: **thin bone strokes**.

A fine red-brown haired brush can also be used for even finer control of a line, as required for leaf and flower veins: **elongated hook and needle strokes**; pine leaves and seaweed:

fine needle strokes; water lines: **fine orchid leaf strokes**, and for detailing of stamen and pollen dots. It is also the ideal brush for outlining strokes, which need to be as fine as taut wire.

Use an old red-haired brush for dry brush work when a rough appearance is required.

White Brush (goat-hair)—*absorbent*—Holds a plentiful amount of water needed for large strokes or when a number of strokes are put together to make one larger form. It is useful for the **teardrop and spot strokes** as used for the petals of flowers where soft faded edges are required.

The Loading of the Brush

Always load the wetter, lighter tone first so that it absorbs to the base of the hairs. Add about an equal amount of water to the colour mentioned in the text to dilute the paint to a smooth consistency. The thicker, darker tone is added last on to the tip of the hairs. The second colour is used with no added water or just a little if required for ease of application.

Sometimes the brush is loaded with water before adding the colour, then the brush is dipped in the water container and excess water wiped off on the edge of the container.

If it indicates in the text that two colours are to be mixed, then equal amounts of both colours are blended together on the palette before being loaded on to the brush.

If one colour is to be toned with another, the first mentioned colour has just enough of the second colour added to it to change its tone (shade) but not enough to produce a third colour: usually the proportions will be 2:1.

The exact amount of water and colour depends on many factors, including size of the brush, size of the stroke, wetness required, absorbency of the paper or silk being used, etc. Only experience and practice will bring the sensitivity required to produce the desired effect.

When the brush is used upright the darker colour will come out first and then the lighter colour, forming strokes of diminishing tones.

When the brush is used on an angle the two colours will come out beside each other forming double-toned strokes. The lower the angle of the brush the thicker the stroke and the more colour released from the brush.

After some practice at producing the various strokes there will come an ability to translate a Chinese painting into the movements used by the artist, bringing an appreciation of the internal rhythmic qualities of the work. This enhances the viewing of a finished work, for its own visual satisfaction or for the reproduction of an example.

On the illustrations the arrows indicate the direction of the stroke. The arrow head is at the finish of each stroke and any numbers are at the beginning of each stroke. Where either end of the directional arrow is curved around, as in the bone or teardrop strokes, this indicates that an increase in pressure is to be applied.

Following are five basic strokes with some of their variations, to cover the range used in this book. There are seven basic strokes with—depending on the classification—some forty variations in Chinese calligraphy. In painting the variations are as infinite as nature.

Dot Strokes

Use a white-haired brush on an angle: the larger the stroke the lower the angle.

FIG. 1 Load the brush first with a light blue mixed with a small amount of water (cerulean or cobalt blues are used in this book). To the tip of the brush add a little purple of thicker paint.

Each colour should be clearly seen as separate on the brush, and then it will appear so on the paper. This principle applies to all types of double loading of the brush.

Begin at the top left of the stroke, and keep both the fingers holding the brush and the wrist still. Use a whole arm movement to pull the brush down, around and back up to the starting point and keep the tip of the brush pointing to the left of the stroke, to form a firm edged circle as for the grapes. This principle of holding the brush still and painting with the whole arm applies to all of the paintings, except very small strokes where the wrist or fingers can be moved.

The darker colour (purple) of each stroke will show the movement of the tip of the brush. The lighter edge (blue) shows the movement of the hairs at the base of the brush. This is so for all of the brush strokes.

Fig. 2 The brush is first loaded with water, then light blue three-quarters up the brush and tipped in purple.

Lay the brush at a lower angle than for the previous stroke, using a similar movement to produce a soft edge to the stroke, indicative of the fragility of petals, as for hydrangea or wisteria. Again the tip of the brush remains on the left side of the stroke.

Fig. 3 First place light blue on the whole brush, and then purple up to half way. A larger more oval stroke is produced by moving the stroke around a central space. This can be left or filled in by returning the brush over it in a second downward movement, as for the grapes in Chapter 19 Fig. 1. (p. 124).

Fig. 4 A broader, longer stroke, which is oval. The brush is loaded with sap green then tipped in black. After the first central stroke is completed, if all the black has been painted out of the brush as is usually the case, retip the brush in black and paint another slightly smaller stroke on the left side of the first stroke. Add a third stroke on the right of the first stroke. This forms a single leaf with three rounded lobes, as for the grape leaf. This introduces the technique of placing a number of strokes together to produce one larger form.

Fig. 5 With a fine brush loaded with black, apply the tip to the paper and then lift the brush up again to produce a small dot suitable for the pollen of flowers, the eye of a bird or moss on a branch (make sure it appears round and not triangular).

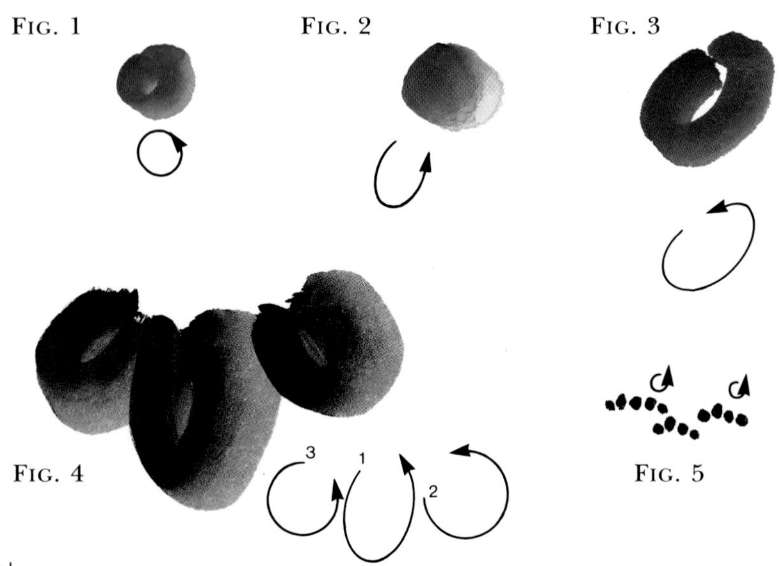

Fig. 1 Fig. 2 Fig. 3

Fig. 4 Fig. 5

Bone Strokes

Fig. 6a Use the fine brush, held upright and loaded with sap green and tipped in black. Press the tip of the brush on to the paper and then lift it up again, but not completely off the paper. Pull the brush down and along the paper stopping at the required length. Press down again and then lift the brush up and off the paper as it is pulled back over the stroke for a rounded end.

The basic bone stroke is on the far left, beside this are variations of this stroke used for stems. Each is in one continuous line. With a complete arm movement from the shoulder, glide the small finger, or the wrist of the painting hand, along the surface of the paper to help steady the brush.

Fig. 6b If at the end of a bone stroke the brush is not pulled back over the end of the stroke but is lifted gradually off to one side and then back as it is lifted off the paper, the point will be exposed producing a hook stroke (which is the next stroke).

Fig. 6c Construction of hook strokes for veins of a leaf. With a fine brush loaded with black, first paint the central stroke then the strokes either side, working down and out from the central stroke.

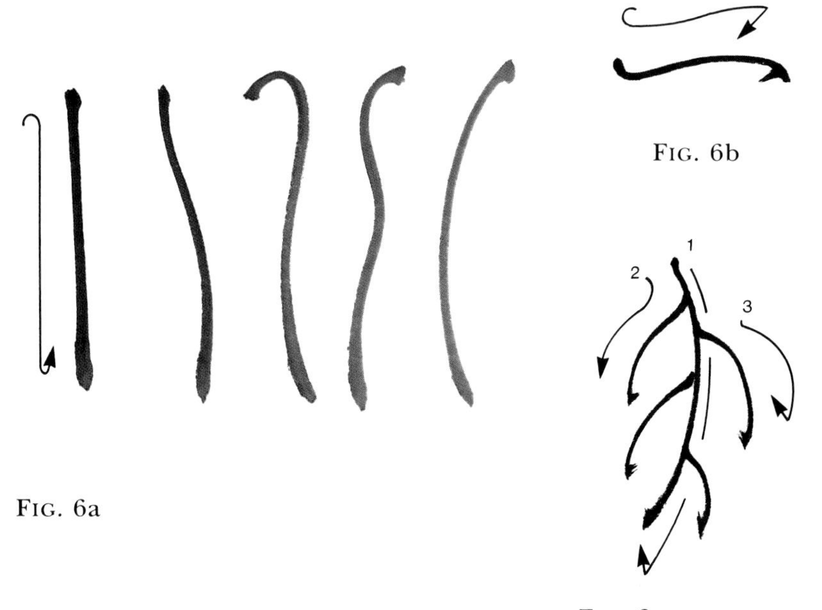

Fig. 6b

Fig. 6a

Fig. 6c

Fig. 7 Vines are good practice for one continuous movement and steady line technique. They have either a round end (bone stroke) or a pointed end (needle stroke).

Fig. 8 With a white-haired brush loaded with sap green and tipped in black, with the brush held on an angle of about 45°, paint a wide bone stroke (the largest, darkest stroke seen in the example). Without retipping the brush, paint a series of bone strokes of decreasing length on the right side of the first stroke, then add some more bone strokes of even less length on the left side of the first stroke. This forms a lotus leaf and practises the principle of using a number of strokes to make one form.

Fig. 9 Use an old red-haired brush loaded with burnt sienna mixed with a little indigo and tipped in black, then dab the brush on a cotton cloth to absorb some of the water. Hold the brush at an angle with the tip of the brush pointed away from the body. Paint a bone stroke, quickly and with little pressure, but still with both ends of the stroke thicker, to produce a dry, rugged effect. If the first stroke does not have the desired streaks of white in it, then paint more bone strokes with the same loaded brush until the brush is sufficiently dry to produce them. Use this stroke to form branches, first the main branch then the side branches out from it. The same principles of construction used for the leaf veins apply.

Needle Strokes

Fig. 10 Use a red-haired brush, held upright and loaded with sap green and tipped in indigo. Press the tip of the brush down on to the paper and then lift the brush up slightly. Pull the brush along to the right, lifting it smoothly up and gradually off the paper. Continue to move the brush after it has left the surface of the paper to produce a fine point to finish off the stroke. This is a bamboo leaf and also forms the body of a fish. It is the hardest of the strokes to do.

To achieve the point in this stroke and the orchid leaf stroke, the tip of the brush will need to be pointed by stroking

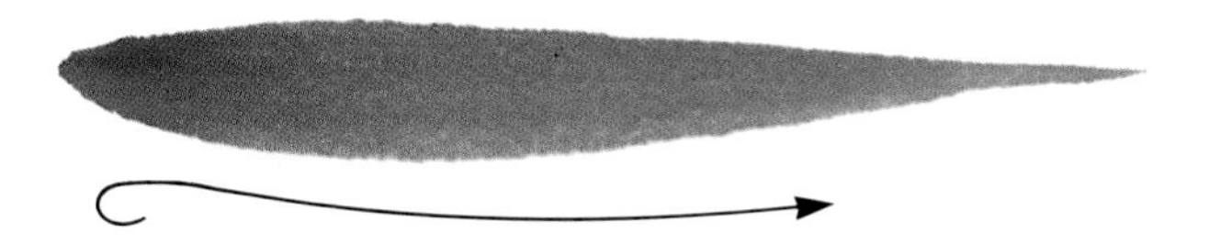

the hairs on the palette. Hold the brush on an angle and turn it so that each side of the brush gathers paint and the hairs are shaped into a fine point. After one or two strokes the brush may need to be repointed. With practice many strokes can be painted without repointing the brush. Do not twist the brush as this will tangle the hairs and split the point; keep the hairs parallel with each other.

FIG. 11a Paint a shorter version with the brush loaded with light blue and tipped in purple.

FIG. 11b With the brush on an angle of 45° and the tip of the brush pointed away from the body, paint a short, thick needle stroke. This technique is also used for the body of a fish.

FIG. 11a FIG. 11b

FIG. 12a With the brush loaded with sap green and tipped in black, held at angle of 45° with the tip pointed to the left, paint a thick downward needle stroke.

FIG. 12b Slightly curve the stroke out at the middle and place a second stroke beside it. The second stroke curves in the opposite direction to form a symmetrical, rounded leaf. One of the two strokes comes to a point to form a sharp tipped leaf. If the gap in the middle is too large a third stroke can be applied to fill it in. This technique is used for many wide leaves such as hydrangea and hibiscus, or with variation in the middle movement of the stroke as for pansy leaves.

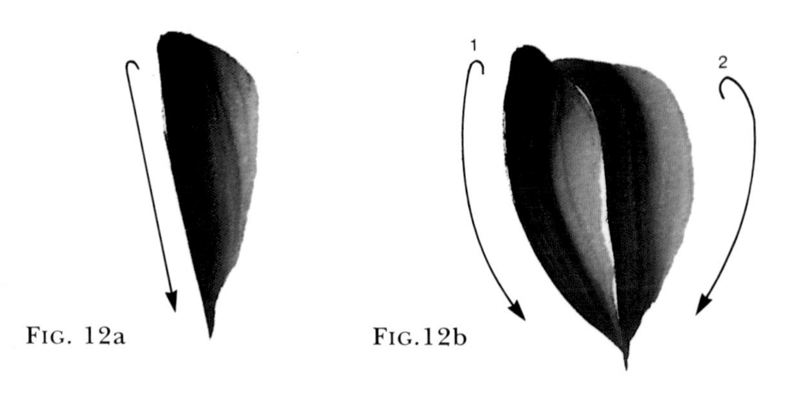

FIG. 12a FIG.12b

Fig. 13a With an upright fine brush loaded with sap green tipped in black, paint a thin needle stroke as the central stroke of a pine leaf cluster.

Fig. 13b Add similar side strokes alternating left then right down the stem. Each stroke is painted towards the stem.

Fig. 13c This same fine, elongated stroke, with a slight curve at its start, can be used to form another type of leaf vein. Paint the central stroke first and then the side strokes.

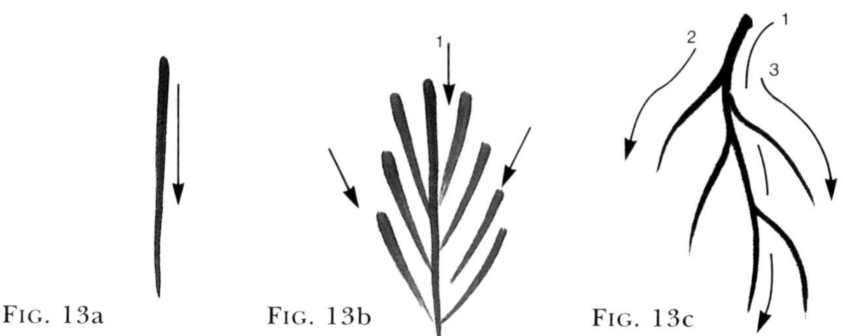

Fig. 13a Fig. 13b Fig. 13c

Fig. 14a Use a shorter fine needle stroke for the seaweed.

Fig. 14b Paint a number of strokes in a group with a common centre. Begin with the middle stroke.

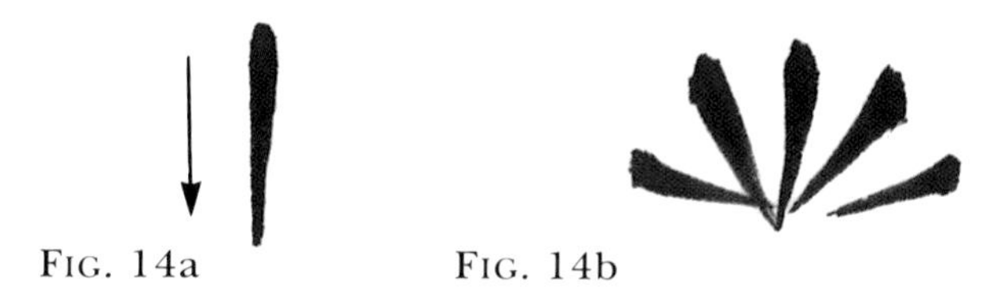

Fig. 14a Fig. 14b

Teardrop Strokes

Fig. 15 Load a white-haired brush with water then alizarin crimson and tip in purple. Hold the brush upright

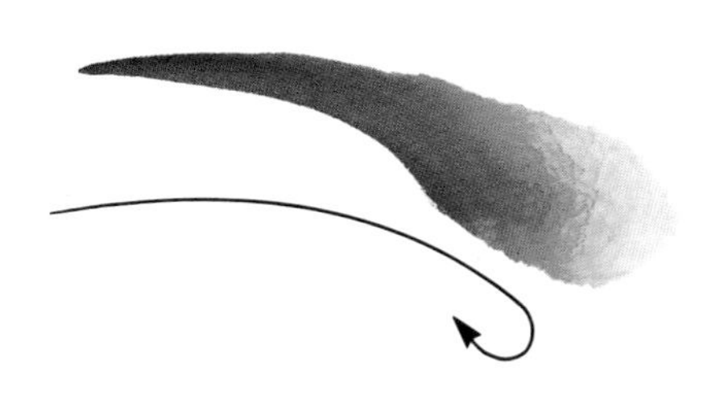

and off the paper. Move the brush slowly down and along, left to right, until it touches the paper. Gradually apply more pressure to increase the thickness of the stroke while the brush still moves, to produce a tapered beginning. At the finish of the stroke press the full extent of the brush on to the paper to discharge the water from the base of the hairs for a soft, and by pulling the brush back over the stroke, rounded end. This is used for long petals such as for the poppy. It is a reverse movement to the needle stroke.

Fig. 16 A variation of the teardrop stroke with a curved beginning, with the brush loaded with yellow and tipped in rose madder. Where the colours merge an orange tone is produced, which is used for the tail of the goldfish.

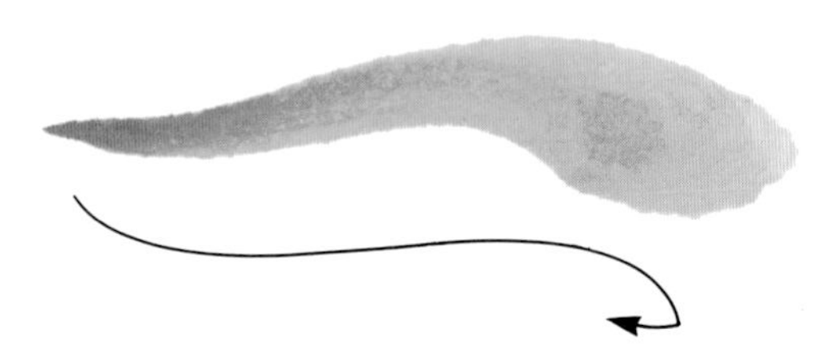

Fig. 17 A number of the above strokes placed together to form one large lobed petal. In an actual painting the strokes would slightly overlap and merge together to make one form. Here they are separated for clarity. Paint the strokes in the order shown. This stroke is used to form a hibiscus petal.

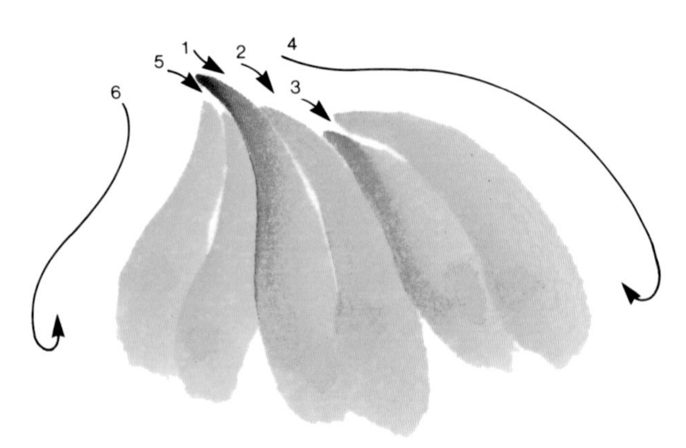

Fig. 18 Use a red-haired brush loaded with sap green tipped in indigo and paint a number of short teardrop strokes. This stroke is used to form most calyxes and for very small young leaves.

Fig. 19 Use a red-haired brush loaded with sap green and tipped in indigo to paint an extended curved beginning to this teardrop stroke, which is used for another type of seaweed.

Orchid Leaf Strokes

Fig. 20a Use a red-haired brush, held upright and loaded with sap green and tipped in black. Begin the stroke as for the teardrop stroke but instead of finishing with more pressure for a rounded end, slowly begin to lift the brush up at the thick middle of the stroke and keep it moving steadily as it is brought completely off the paper, forming a pointed tip. Finish with a follow through movement as for the finish of the needle stroke. This is a soft stroke, thin at both ends: an opposite movement to the bone stroke.

Figs. 20b, 20c Variations of the orchid leaf stroke with a slight curve in the middle of the stroke. For small leaves as on the bellflower.

Fig. 20a

Fig. 20b

Fig. 20c

Fig. 21 For a more complex leaf begin with a central curved orchid leaf stroke. Add shorter side strokes out from the central leaf to form a pointed serrated leaf. This stroke is used for the poppy leaf.

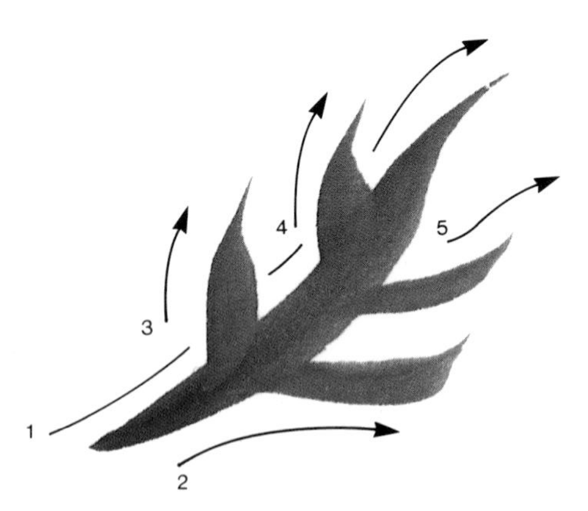

Fig. 22a With the brush loaded with yellow and tipped in rose madder, hold the brush at angle of 45° with the tip pointed to the left and paint a downward orchid leaf stroke.

Fig. 22b Add a second stroke to the right of the first with the central portion curved in the opposite direction to form a symmetrical rounded petal that has a pointed tip and base. This stroke is used for the lotus petal. Notice the similarities and the differences to the leaf in Fig. 12b (p. 16).

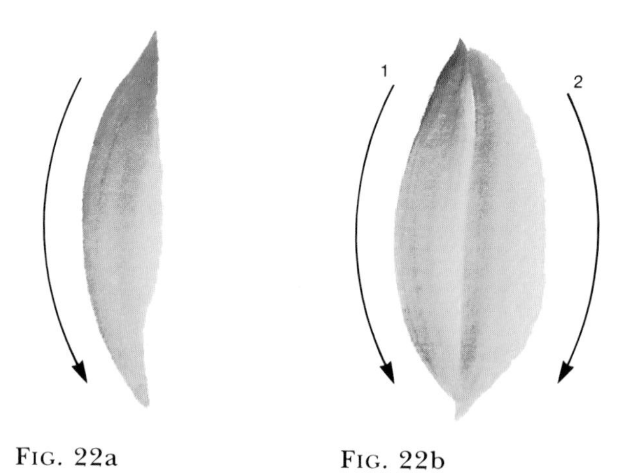

Fig. 22a Fig. 22b

Fig. 23 With a fine brush, loaded with burnt sienna mixed with indigo and tipped in black, paint a short downward bone stroke for the stem of a pine cone. Working left to right, paint a series of fine orchid leaf strokes from the stem down to the tip of the cone.

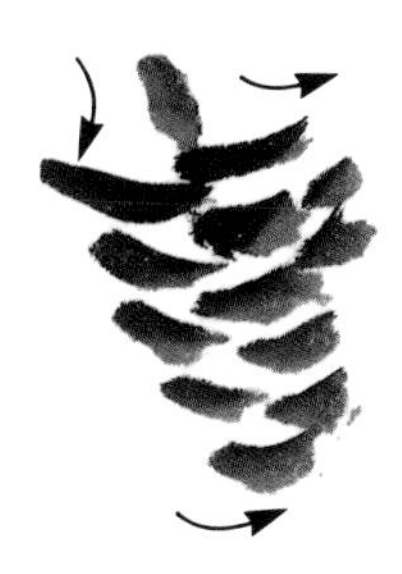

Water

Fig. 24a Use a fine brush loaded with a diluted mixture of light blue toned with a little indigo and paint a long fine orchid leaf stroke as the basic water line.

Fig. 24b A variation produced by alternatively increasing and decreasing the pressure on the brush as it is moved along to produce an undulating movement.

Fig. 24c A thicker water stroke.

Fig. 25a A pattern of flowing water using a fine curved leaf stroke.

Fig. 25b A pattern of calmer water using a straight stroke.

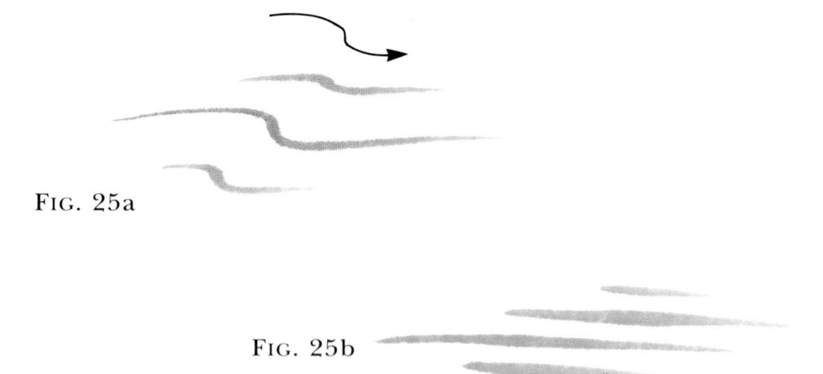

Fig. 25a

Fig. 25b

The following chapters present various subjects to develop the techniques and are in order of degree of difficulty. Often the techniques for a particular chapter are built upon those of an earlier one, so it is best to proceed through the exercises without missing any. Later more time can be given to the perfecting of those subjects that you are most interested in.

As a guide to the practical aspects of learning through painting, first look at the finished composition that you are about to paint. Study all its visual elements separately. Interpret the brush strokes and colours used. Appreciate the inseparable interrelationship of all the strokes and elements to form the composition as a whole unit.

If you do not have some knowledge of the appearance of the subject try to view it in nature. If this is not possible, because of season or location, study from photographs. Next, read the instructions and complete any intermediate exercises, referring to the finished composition as needed. Read any additional instructions for the finished composition before proceeding to paint it. Always follow the instructions in the order specified, referring back to the instructions as needed.

It is easier to paint larger than smaller, so paint the examples at least as large as they are shown. If there is difficulty in placing all of the elements on the paper then paint even larger, especially for the more complex compositions, which have been painted larger and reduced to fit the book.

Place the example you are working from as close as practical to the paper you are copying it on to.

For the purpose of learning the techniques try to closely copy the example you are working from. Distinguish between the essentials that need to be exact and those that do not matter. For example, it is important to achieve the correct brush stroke and to use the correct tones to express the appropriate character, but the exact colour or position of the subject may not be so important as they may vary in nature.

Paint those pictures that you enjoy most a number of times so that the techniques and the spirit of the painting become absorbed into your heart, then you will find that you can do free interpretations of that theme. That is the first step before working from the subject using nature as your teacher. First absorb all the lessons in the examples and in the subject, so that painting can flow direct from the image in the heart, which is a reflection of the harmonious universe.

The expression of mood through traditional floral seasonal symbols reflects the oneness with nature aspired to by the artist.

Winter	—	Pine	—	Vigour
Spring	—	Wisteria	—	Rebirth
Summer	—	Willow	—	Gentleness
Autumn	—	Grapes	—	Abundance

CHAPTER 5

PINE TREE

The pine tree, with its strong, gnarled branches and its evergreen leaves, is representative of winter and the hardy persevering qualities of long life.

Used as the most common tree in landscape painting, the pine is shown in close detail and can later be used as a complement to the softer aspects of flowers and birds. It teaches the techniques necessary for producing branches and fine resilient leaves. Before starting the exercises refer to Fig. 4 for the completed composition.

FIG. 1 Begin at the base of the main branch with a bone stroke as described in Chapter 4 Fig. 9 (p. 15). Use a white-haired brush loaded with burnt sienna mixed with indigo to produce a deep tone of brown. Black is added to the tip of the brush.

Paint all of the main branch then the side branches, adding them from the main branch out to the tip. Make sure that they are attached firmly to the main branch by slightly overlapping them on to it. Paint quickly with light pressure for a dry brush effect.

Fig. 2 Add the leaves with a fine needle stroke as described in Chapter 4 Fig. 13a (p. 17). A red-haired brush is loaded with sap green mixed with indigo then tipped in black. The consistency of the paint is wetter than for the branch to produce a smooth, flexible stroke.

Paint the centre stem of the leaves from its tip to its base then add a line of needle strokes at angle of 45° to the main stem. Start with the topmost leaf and work down the stem. Add a second layer of leaves at an angle of about 60°. In later compositions up to four layers at different angles can be added.

Fig. 3 The pine cone is painted with a series of short orchid leaf strokes, as fully described in Chapter 4 Fig. 23 (p. 21).

Fig. 4 In the finished composition no two leaf groups are parallel to each other. Also observe the placement of the negative areas (white spaces of paper) to create an asymmetrical but harmoniously balanced design. The posture of this composition reflects a stretching gesture.

FIG. 5 The leaf pattern in the composition of Fig. 6 is constructed differently from that of Fig. 4, but the strokes and the colours are the same. Begin at the centre of each group. The exact number of needles is not important. This is as described in Chapter 4 Fig. 14b (p. 17).

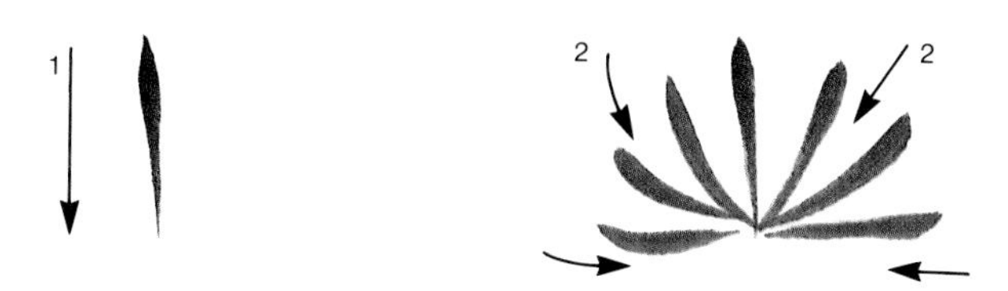

FIG. 6 In the finished composition overlap each group to form a dense mass of leaves.

Each leaf group does not have to be attached to a branch as long as they are joined to another group. The branches and leaves are formed around a central space to form an image of an embracing gesture.

CHAPTER 6

BELLFLOWER

This simple flower teaches the principles for the construction of all flowers and uses the teardrop stroke to make pointed petals. Refer to Fig. 9 for the finished composition.

Begin with the buds.

FIG. 1 Load a white-haired brush with a medium amount of water then add light blue to the lower half of the hairs and tip in purple. Paint a teardrop stroke as described in Chapter 4 Fig. 18 (p. 19). Here it is a little larger.

FIG. 2 The stroke for the bud can also be used as the first petal of the flower. Paint the other petals in the order shown. This is a simple method of achieving a symmetrical placement of five petals, allowing the other two petals to be placed in the spaces left.

Adjust the position of the hand and the brush for each petal, keeping the tip of the brush pointed out from the centre of the flower as indicated by the arrows. This will give pointed, deep coloured tips and a soft faded centre formed by the water at the base of the hairs of the brush.

FIG. 1

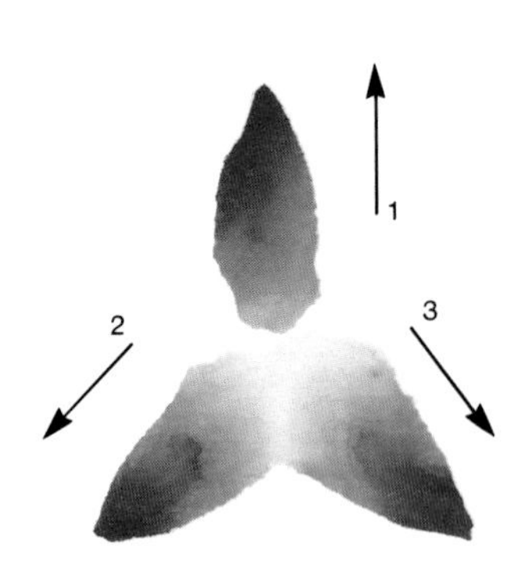

FIG. 2

Fig. 3 When placing in the last two petals, leave a space of white paper at the centre to form the 'face' of the flower.

Fig. 4 Add the throat of the flower in two short, fine bone strokes painted away from the flower in the direction of the arrows towards where the stem will be.

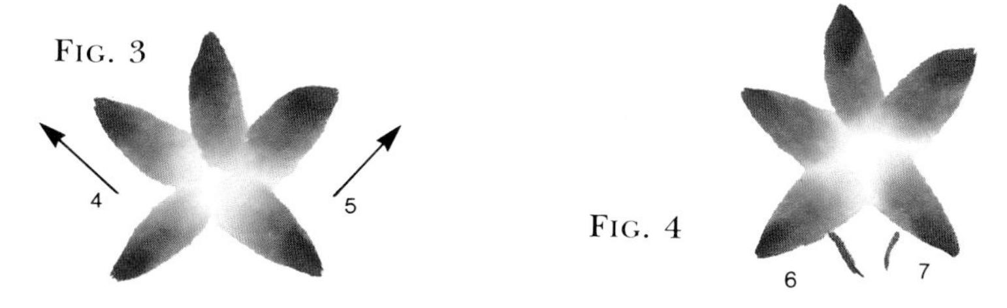

Fig. 3 Fig. 4

Fig. 5 With a red-haired brush held upright and loaded with wet black paint add the calyxes in short, dark teardrop strokes under the base of the buds and flowers. With the same loaded brush use a long fine bone stroke for the stem. Paint from under the calyx to the ground.

Chinese flower painting is always of the living plant. The stem must be attached firmly into the earth.

Fig. 6 Reload the red-haired brush with a light grey (black diluted with water) and use short orchid strokes for the leaves as shown in Chapter 4 Fig. 20a (p. 19). The direction of the arrow is the direction of the stroke.

Begin with the longer, darker leaves that are lower down the stem and are painted outwards. As the black on the brush runs out, paint the younger leaves in a medium grey near the top of the stem and inward. The leaves are alternate not opposing, that is, each leaf starts at a different point on the stem: no two leaves grow from the same point.

Fig. 5 Fig. 6

Fig. 7 Add a centre with a dot stroke using a white-haired brush loaded with yellow and tipped in red. Make sure that the flower petals are dry to avoid bleeding of colours.

Fig. 8 When the centre is dry use a fine brush, loaded with alizarin crimson (a deep red) to paint the stamens in short, sharp needle strokes. These are the features of the 'face'.

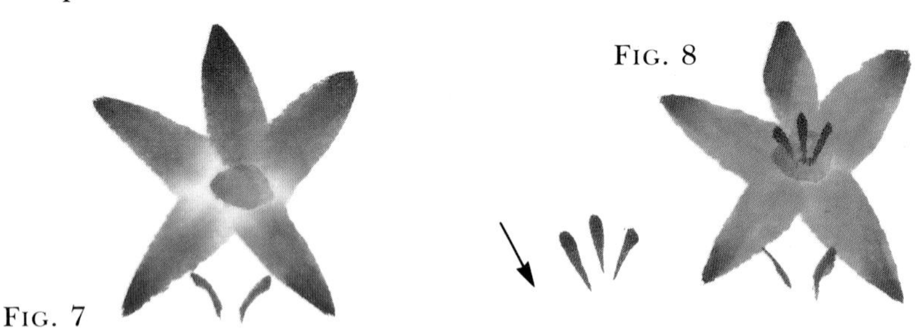

Fig. 7 Fig. 8

Fig. 9 A completed composition.

Paint the buds then the flowers facing in different directions. The brush may need to be reloaded after the first flower and repointed on the palette. Add the calyxes then paint the stems of the flowers before the stems of the buds. These stems appear to go *behind* the flower to help push the flower forward (this technique is called underlapping). White spaces are formed between the lines of the stems and the flowers; these are the 'eyes' of the composition so don't make them too pinched and narrow. Next, add the leaves: their directions are important in producing the rhythm of the painting. Add the centres and the stamens of the flowers. These will help to face the flowers in different directions.

FIG. 10 A more complex arrangement of flowers.

There are many white spaces formed by the intersecting of stems and flowers.

Let the flowers dance on the breeze.

CHAPTER 7

GRAPES

The portrayal of fruit and vegetables also comes under the classification of flowers. The formation of a cabbage is as beautiful as that of a rose. Fruit is respected not only as a source of nourishment but also as a symbol of the profligacy of propagation.

May your children's children be many.

Refer to Fig. 7 for the completed composition.

FIG. 1 Begin with the fruit. Load a white-haired brush with sap green and tip in purple. Paint a round dot stroke as described in Chapter 4 Fig. 1 (p. 11).

FIG. 2 Add other grapes in an offset pattern, like bricks in a wall.

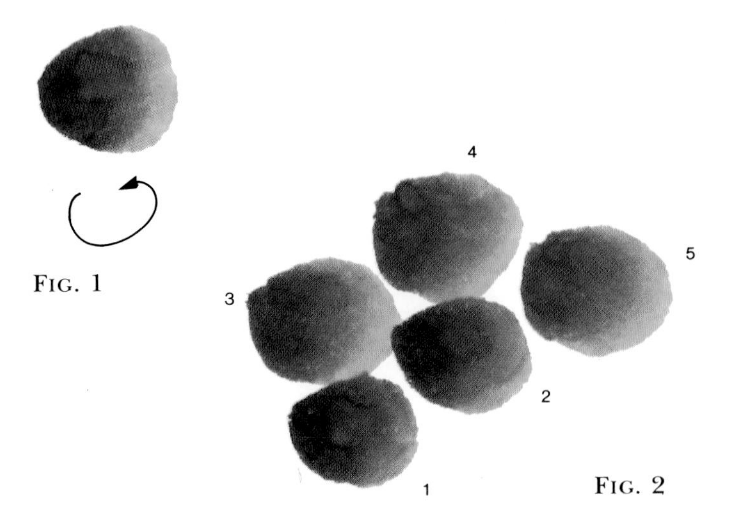

FIG. 1

FIG. 2

Fig. 3 The completed bunch of grapes is not too symmetrical. Add the stems in sap green tipped in indigo, with short bone strokes. There is a main stem that branches out to both sides.

Fig. 4 Begin the first lobe of the leaf with a white-haired brush, loaded with sap green tipped in black. Use a large elongated round stroke. Refer to Chapter 4 Fig. 4 (p. 12).

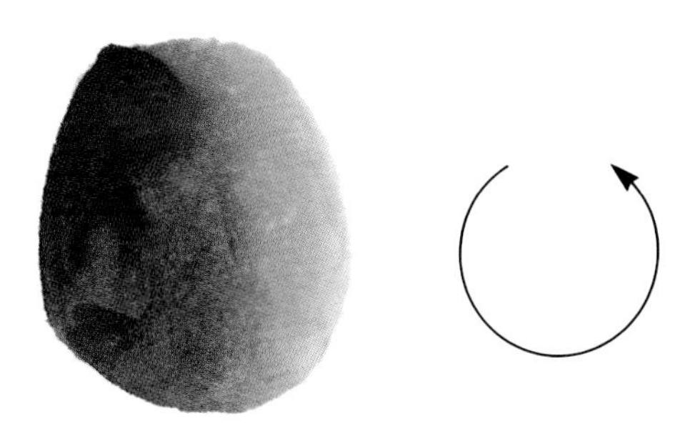

Fig. 5 Add the other lobes of the leaf with similar strokes in the order shown. They become smaller towards the back of the leaf. Paint the whole leaf with the one load of the brush. It is a five lobed leaf.

Next add the branch as for the pine tree.

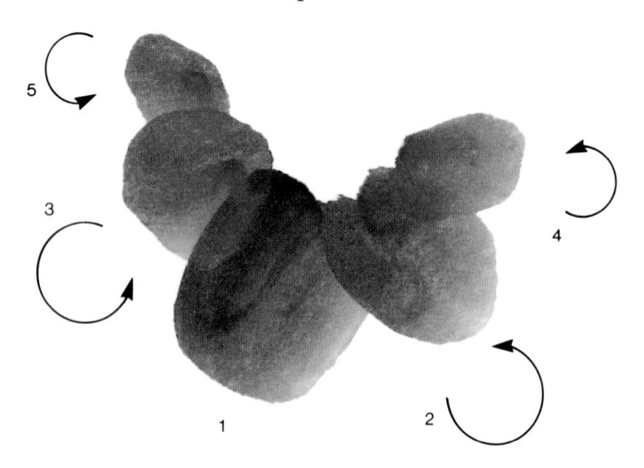

Fig. 6a, 6b Paint the vine with fine curved bone strokes that still remain taut. Keep the brush upright to control the evenness of line. Rest the small finger or the wrist of the painting hand on the paper to steady the brush if needed. Refer to Chapter 4 Fig. 7 (p. 14).

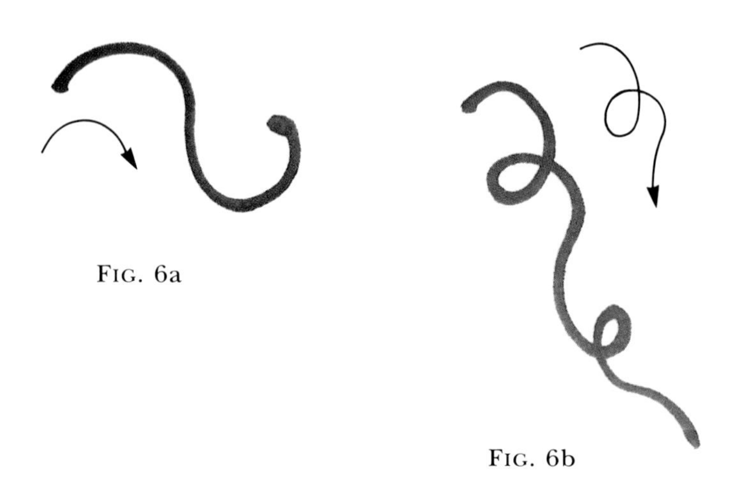

Fig. 6a

Fig. 6b

FIG. 7 The completed composition.

Begin with the grapes then the leaves, the younger leaf is in sap green tipped in red, then add the branch, then the details of stem, vine and small black dots to face the fruit. These do not appear in nature but give character to the main subject (host).

Fig. 8 A more complex composition.

Most of the compositional elements are grouped along the top and down the right edge, placing the visual weight in one corner, retaining plenty of space for the movement of the eye through the composition. This way the picture does not seem congested.

CHAPTER 8

POPPY

罌粟

This is a winter flower. Its bright, red colour warms the heart on a dull and cold day.

The techniques of this subject are extensions of those used for the bellflower in Chapter 6. The petal stroke is longer, the leaves are serrated but the stem and the stamens are the same.

Refer to Fig. 8 for the completed composition.

FIG. 1 Begin with the central lobe of the front petal of the flower. Use a white-haired brush, loaded with plenty of water then with alizarin crimson to halfway up the hairs and tipped in purple. Paint a long teardrop stroke as in Chapter 4 Fig. 15 (p. 17). The brush is laid quite low on the paper to allow the water on the base of the hairs to form a soft edge to the petal.

FIG. 2 To the central lobe add a shorter lobe on each side to form a petal of three lobes.

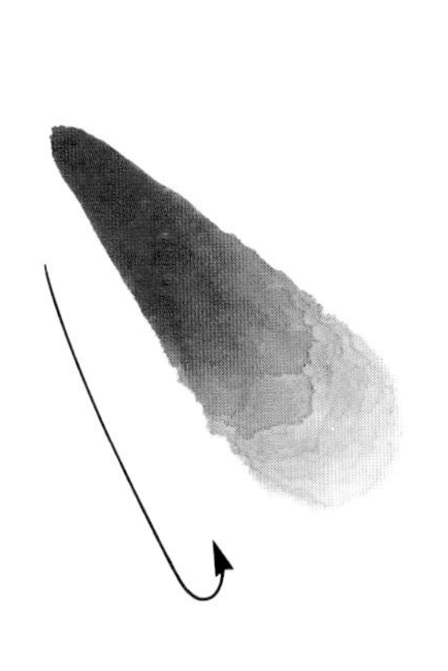

FIG. 1

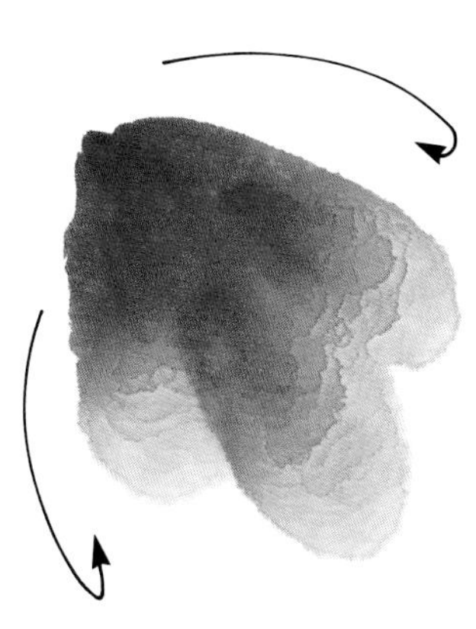

FIG. 2

Fig. 3 The poppy is a four petalled flower. Add each petal in the order shown. For each stroke keep the tip of the brush pointed towards the centre of the flower as indicated by the arrows. Try to complete the entire flower with the one load of paint on the brush, but if the brush needs to be reloaded with any or all of the colours take care to obtain a similar tone. The point of the brush may need to be repointed after a few strokes.

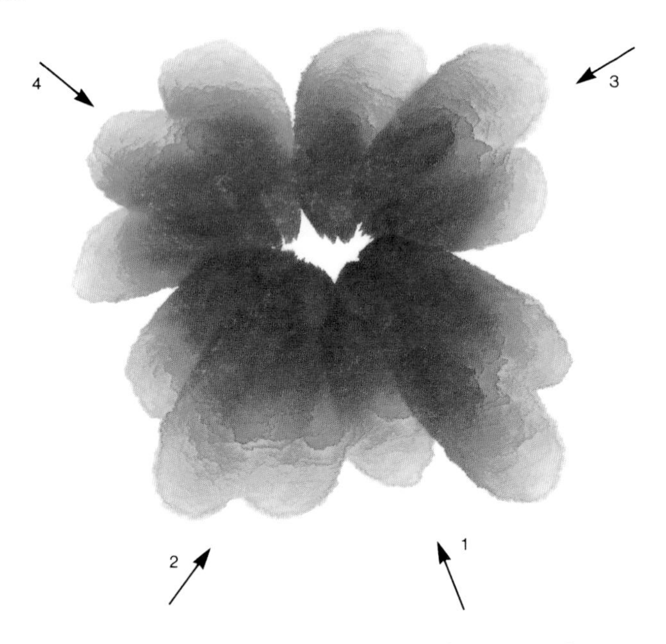

Fig. 4 The buds are painted in two short teardrop strokes without laying the brush down enough for the soft water edge to appear.

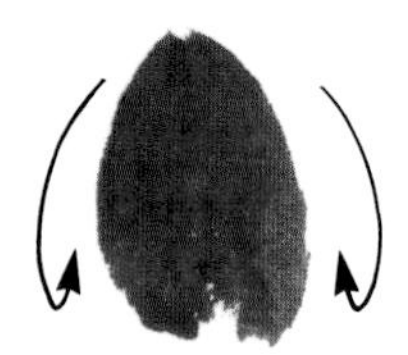

Fig. 5 With a red-haired brush loaded with sap green and tipped in indigo add a calyx to each bud in two short teardrop strokes. Point the tip of the brush in the direction of the arrows.

Add the stem with the same brush but with it held upright. Begin at the base of the flower and paint a thicker section in two strokes to hold the large, floppy flower on to the stem. With a long, slightly curved bone stroke bring the stem to the ground. The stem should not be too stiff and should bend at least twice. If the line of the stem is not even enough then check that the brush is being held upright. Do not apply too much pressure and use the small finger of the painting hand to guide by.

Fig. 6 Add the leaves with a red-haired brush using an orchid leaf stroke. Refer to Chapter 4 Fig. 21 (p. 20). The leaves grow at the base of the stems.

For the older leaves, load the brush with sap green and tip in black. Begin with the central section of the leaf, from the base to the tip in the direction of the arrow. Add two shorter sections near the base of the leaf, painted from the leaf out. Then add smaller divisions from these and add some more near the tip of the leaf.

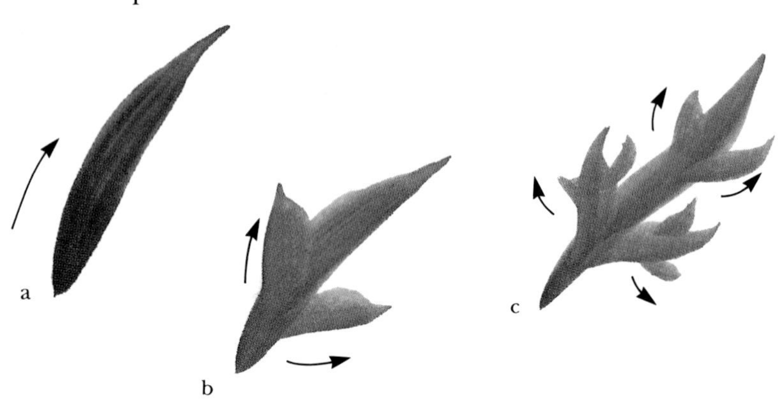

Fig. 7 For young leaves, load the brush with sap green and tip in red. Still use the orchid leaf stroke. Paint the central section from the tip to the base as indicated by the arrow. Add the divisions near the tip of the leaf, then add the lower divisions to complete the leaf. All the strokes are painted towards the base of the leaf.

Fig. 8 A completed composition.

Paint the flower, then the buds, the calyxes and the stems. Then add the leaves—first the older, darker ones (for one of these leaves the brush has been loaded with sap green and tipped in indigo) and last the young red-tipped one.

When the flower is dry add a green dot for the centre knob (mix sap green with a little yellow). Add the stamens with short needle strokes in black.

Fig. 9 For a side view of a poppy, paint the front two petals as for the back two petals of the previous face-on flower.

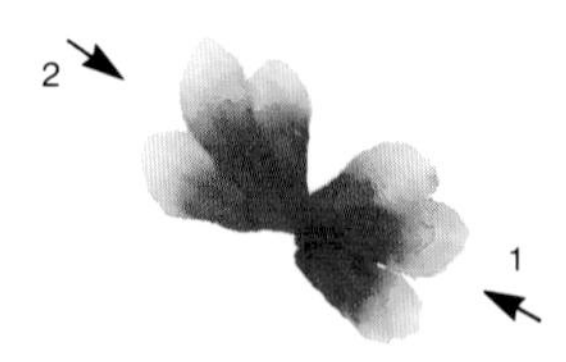

Fig. 10 Above the first two petals paint two more, similar but slightly smaller. For each petal the tip of the brush is pointed towards the base of the petal as indicated by the arrows.

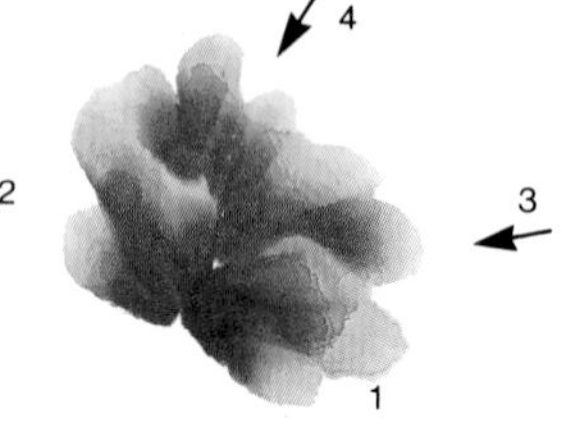

Fig. 11 A more complex composition incorporating side-view flowers.

CHAPTER 9

HYDRANGEA

紫陽花

This subject extends the techniques learnt in the grape composition. Refer to Fig. 7 for the complete composition.

FIG. 1 With a white-haired brush loaded with water, then light blue and tipped in purple, paint a single petal with a large round dot stroke as described in Chapter 4 Fig. 2 (p. 12). Make sure that the soft water edge shows the gentleness of the petal.

FIG. 2 Each flower is made up of four petals painted in the order shown.

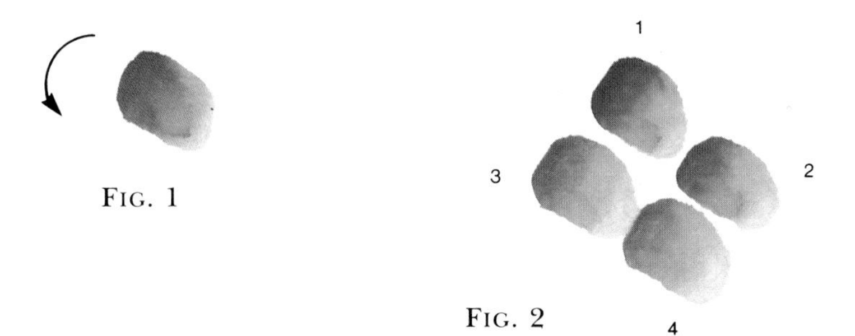

FIG. 1

FIG. 2

FIG. 3 Around the central flower place four other flowers as numbered in the example.

Fig. 4 Add more flowers around the first flower, working towards the outside edge of the flower cluster. Sometimes only two or three petals of a flower are shown as the others are behind another flower. The complete flower cluster is painted with the one brush load of paint. The purple will run out first, then as the blue runs out the edge petals will appear soft and faded as the water is drawn from the brush.

Place a black dot, to represent the stamen, in the centre of each flower to distinguish them. The placement of these dots does not have to be too regular.

With an upright red-haired brush loaded with sap green and tipped in indigo, add the stems in short bone strokes. The stems placed between the flowers visually connect them into one cluster gathered towards the branch.

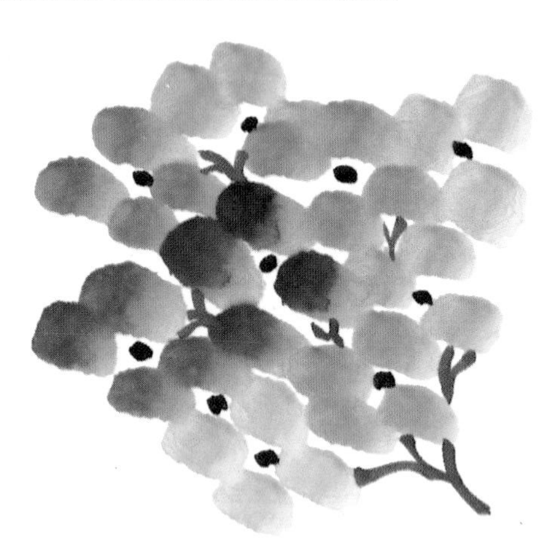

Fig. 5a The leaves are painted with a red-haired brush loaded with sap green and tipped in black. Hold the brush on a low angle and paint a slightly curved needle stroke as shown in Chapter 4 Fig. 12a (p. 16). The leaf is painted from its base to its tip as indicated by the arrow.

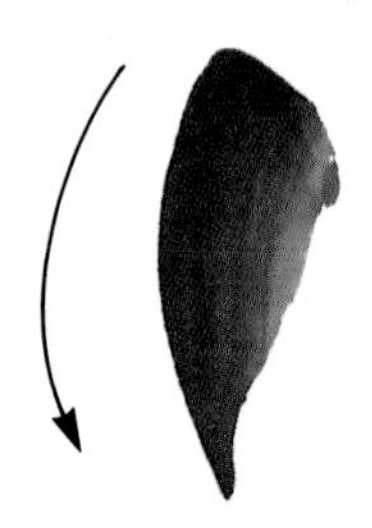

Fig. 5b Add a second stroke beside the first, making sure that one of the two strokes comes to a point.

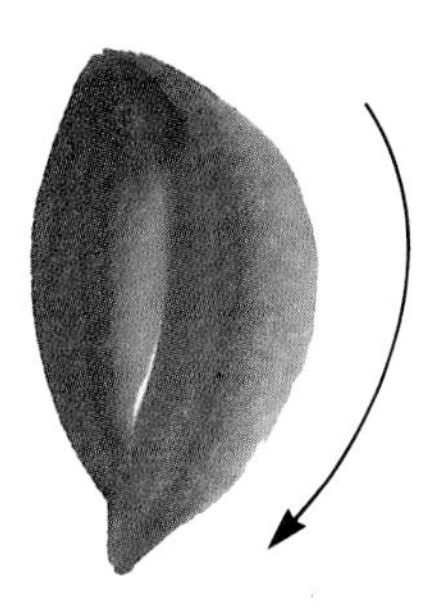

Fig. 6a For the younger leaves load the red-haired brush with sap green and tip in red. Paint the leaf from its tip to its base using an orchid leaf stroke so that the leaf has a red tip, as in nature. Hold the brush on an angle of 45°, as described in Chapter 4 Fig. 22a (p. 20).

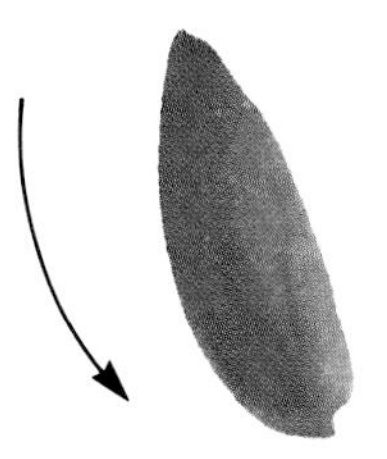

Fig. 6b Add a second stroke to form a complete leaf.

For both these leaves make sure that they have convex sides by making both strokes curve out from the centre line of the leaf. If a gap is left in the middle of the leaf this is most probably because the brush was not held at a low enough angle and so did not form a wide enough stroke. Just fill in the gap with a third stroke.

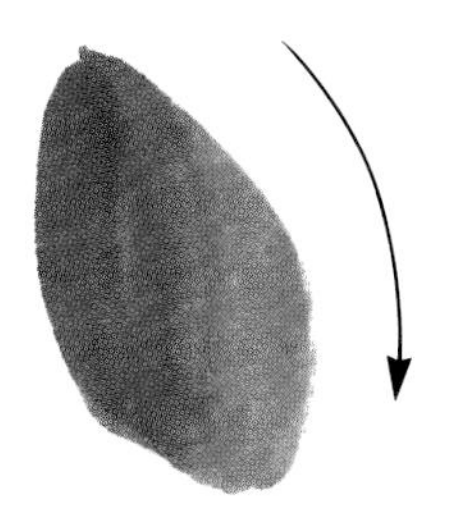

Fig. 7 A completed composition.

Begin with the flower, from the centre of the cluster to the edge. Add the older leaves, some of which are painted in sap green tipped in burnt sienna (brown). Then add the younger leaves. All the leaves are grouped close around the flowers so that they appear to sit on a bed of leaves.

Add the branch as for the pine tree, beginning at the tip of the main branch and going to the base at the edge of the paper. Next add the side branches. With sap green tipped in red add the small leaves on the tip of the branch with a single stroke towards the branch. The stroke is described in Chapter 4 Fig. 18 (p. 19). Add the moss on the branch in black, refer to Chapter 4 Fig. 5 (p. 12). When the flowers are dry, add the centres and the stems.

Fig. 8 For this flower load the white-haired brush with water then halfway with rose madder (pink), or use red diluted with water. Tip in purple. Paint as for the previous flower. Position the flower on the paper so that there is the appropriate space for the later arrival of the butterfly.

Add the leaves. Some are painted in sap green tipped in indigo. The veins on the leaves are added when the leaves are almost dry so that they fade in slightly but do not bleed. For each leaf use a vein colour that is the deepest colour on that leaf. For the green-black leaves use black veins and for the red-green leaves use red veins.

The brush stroke and construction for the veins is described in Chapter 4 Fig. 6b (p. 13).

After adding the branches and the small leaves add the flower centres, stems and the moss.

Add the butterfly, placed so as to be in conversation with the flowers. Its construction is described in Chapter 11 Fig. 9 (p. 58).

CHAPTER 10

WISTERIA

The flowers further develop the dot stroke. The leaf strokes are developed from the bellflower leaves. Fig. 11 shows a completed composition.

FIG. 1 Load a white-haired brush with water then light blue and tip in purple. Paint a large dot stroke as for a hydrangea petal, as in Chapter 4 Fig. 2 (p. 12).

FIG. 2 Paint a second similar stroke to the right of the dot stroke to form the two main petals of the flower.

FIG. 3 Retip the brush in purple and paint two smaller upward strokes at the join of the two larger petals, to form a four petalled flower similar to a sweet-pea.

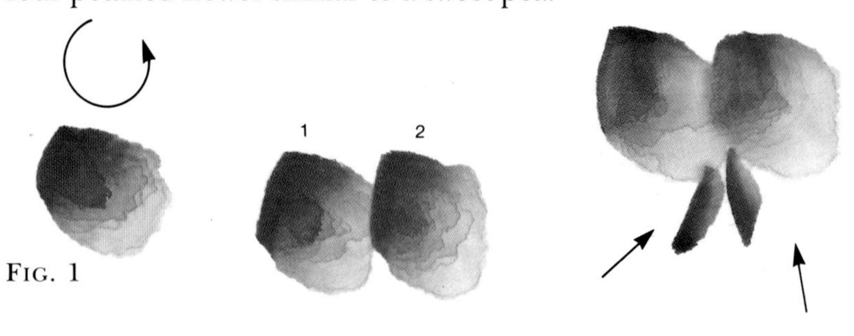

FIG. 1

FIG. 2

FIG. 3

FIG. 4 For a full spray of flowers have the brush well loaded and begin with the buds, painting upwards to the older flowers in the order shown. Paint all the flowers with the one brush load to obtain varying tones, from the darker, firmer buds to the faded older flowers. Retip the brush in purple before adding the centre petals.

With a red-haired brush loaded with sap green and tipped in indigo, paint the stems in a series of short bone strokes, from the top of the spray to the bottom bud. There is one main central stem from which side stems extend to connect all the flowers and buds. Add a spot of white to the inside base of each large petal.

FIG. 5 When the white is dry overlay with gamboge (bright yellow). By placing the white down first as an undercoat the yellow will stand out on the blue, rather than fading in or turning green. This technique for making yellow centres can be applied to other flowers as well.

Fig. 6 For the leaves, load a red-haired brush with sap green tipped in black. Paint a bone stroke for the central stem.

Fig. 7 With an orchid leaf stroke, as shown in Chapter 4 Fig. 20a (p. 19), paint a number of leaves along one side of the stem, beginning with the leaves at the base of the stem. Each leaf is painted out from the stem to its tip.

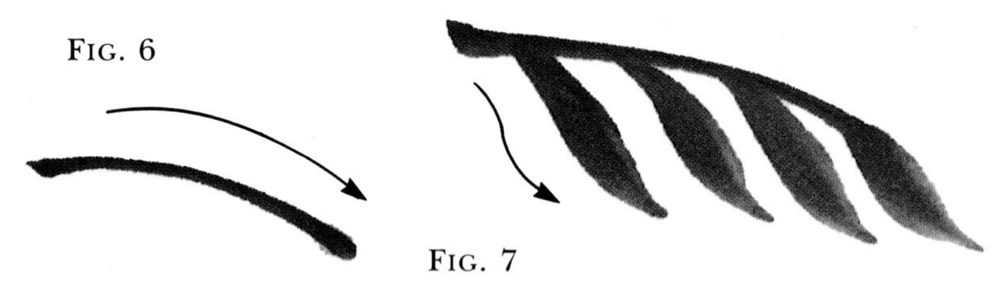
Fig. 6
Fig. 7

Fig. 8 Retip the brush in black before painting the leaves on the other side of the stem, beginning with those at the base of the stem. These leaves oppose each other, that is, they grow in twos, each one from the same point on the stem.

Fig. 9 For younger groups of leaves use sap green tipped in red. They are also painted from their base out to their tip. Begin with the arrowed leaf.

Fig. 8
Fig. 9

Figs. 10a, 10b Using a fine red-haired brush held upright and loaded with sap green tipped in indigo, practise some vines before attempting them in a finished composition. They are more twisted than for the grape vine.

Fig. 11 The completed composition.

Begin with the spray of flowers, then the leaves and connect them together with a branch. This is the same construction order as for the grapes or hydrangea. Add the vines twisting around the branch and extending into the space beneath the flowers. Add the flower stems and centres and then the moss dots.

FIG. 10a
FIG. 10b
FIG. 11

Fig. 12

Fig. 12 Begin with the right hand spray, then the upper left spray, then the leaves, branches, vines with the small leaves added, and then the detail. Keep all these elements to the top and right of the composition to leave plenty of room for the butterfly to flitter about in.

The technique for the butterfly is explained in Chapter 11 Fig. 6 (p. 56).

Open up the gatefold of the front cover for a large composition of a bird and wisteria. Paint the bird first. It is a reverse of Fig. 5, Chapter 18 (p. 118). However, use the colours from the bird in Fig. 3, Chapter 18 (p. 117). Then add the flower groups, then the leaf groups and join them all together with the stems and vines. Note the circular rhythm of the central space formed by the curve of the flower groups.

Now that a number of compositions have been painted a basic pattern for the brush strokes will be seen. Because the brush is always loaded with a light colour before a dark colour the dark colour must come off the brush first producing a brush stroke of dark colour going to light. Therefore not only can the start of each brush stroke be seen, as that is where the darker colour is, but also the order of the strokes can be determined by the diminishing tone.

Thus it becomes possible to read a painting. This will assist in the ease of copying and in following the artist through the movements of the dance of the brush.

CHAPTER 11

BUTTERFLIES

They grace the silent flowers
with their transient presence,
lingering for a moment's conversation.
Then, fluttering on a breeze,
they drift like wind blown petals
to their next destination.

The inclusion of a butterfly produces movement and life in a composition. The dancer has a partner.

When beginning a painting, leave the necessary space for the butterfly, which is added last. It needs room to move about and not feel confined. The flower is the host, the butterfly a passing guest.

The flower and the butterfly can also be painted in the brush style method, but this book concentrates on the outline style, with its refined elegance enhancing the delicacy and impermanence of the butterfly.

FIG. 1 Begin with the body. Use a fine brush loaded with black, hold the brush upright and outline the head in two short and fine curved bone strokes to form a small circle. Two longer bone strokes form an oval for the body (thorax) and a shorter oval for the tail.

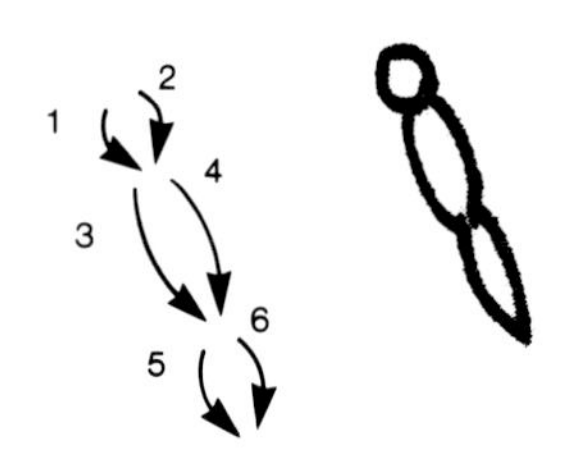

Fig. 2 Add the wings with a fine brush loaded with a light tone of grey (black diluted with water), not too wet or it will give a blurred line.

Begin with the top of the left wing in a long, fine bone stroke out from the top of the thorax, then do the top of the right wing. This will allow you to check visually that the wings are of similar length before adding the rest of the wing. Add the lower line of the wings in a fine scalloped needle stroke. If you are left handed do the right wing first.

Fig. 3 Add the smaller back wings in one stroke each, also using a fine scalloped needle stroke.

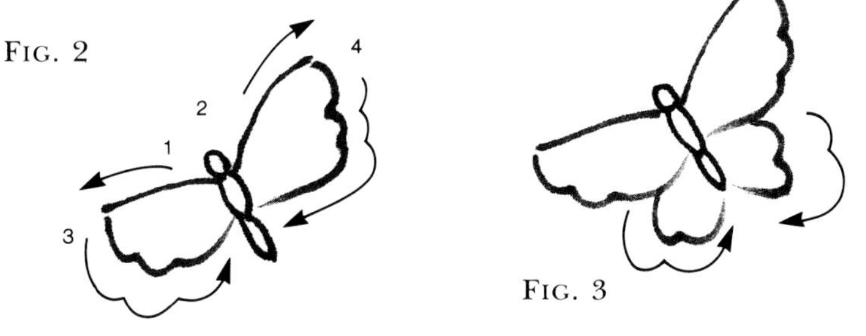

Fig. 4 Now add the colour wash. Use a white-haired brush loaded with sap green and tipped in brown for the body. The wash colours are more diluted than for the brush style strokes. They are light enough not to cover the outline but if they are too diluted they will run over the outline. Practise to control the flow.

For the wings, first place water on the brush then place a small amount of light blue on the tip and lay the brush at a low angle with the tip pointed towards the body of the butterfly. Allow the water to fade the blue towards the edge of the wings. Move quickly, with only a light pressure. For each wing ensure that the brush tip is pointed towards the body for correct tonal effect.

Fig. 5 Add antennae and eyes with a fine brush loaded with indigo mixed with brown. Paint them in towards the body to control their length. Add the wing markings when the wash is almost dry, painting out from the centre, as for the veins on flowers. Use a fine needle stroke of a slightly deeper tone of blue, light blue mixed with a little purple. Use indigo for the body markings. This butterfly is used in Chapter 19 Fig. 5 (p. 131).

Fig. 6 For this butterfly the wash for the wings is first water on the brush then a little yellow and just tipped in red.

The outline of the wings is reinforced with a colour deep enough to cover the grey outline, one reason to keep the first grey outline pale. First add the wash. If it bleeds over the line a little the reinforced colour line will often cover it. In this example the reinforced line is in burnt sienna mixed with a little purple. Also use this mixture for the spots on the wings. The veins are in yellow mixed with red to make an orange tone. This butterfly is used in Chapter 10 Fig. 12 (p. 52).

In all the butterflies illustrated in this chapter, the antennae, eyes and body markings are as described in Fig. 5.

Fig. 7 Here the colour near the body is added first. The brush is loaded with water and tipped in purple. Keep the tip of the brush pointed towards the body. Add the large yellow spots on the front wings. Use burnt sienna tipped in a little indigo to wash in the rest of each wing, from the purple around the yellow to the edge of the wing, with the tip kept pointed towards the body. Retip the brush in indigo before beginning each wing. These three colours, the purple, yellow and brown, respond very well to each other. Add the wing markings in purple. The wing outline is purple mixed with a little brown. This butterfly is used in Chapter 19 Fig. 7 (p. 135).

Fig. 8 For this example, first a wash of water tipped in red is placed on the front wings near the body, then the red dot on each back wing is placed in and then the brown is added to the rest of the wing. The outline is in purple mixed with brown, with the outline for the back wings changing to a contour line, to indicate markings, by varying its thickness. Also outline around the red dots, and add the front wing veins in purple. This butterfly is used in Chapter 19 Fig. 4 (p. 129).

Fig. 9 A wash of water tipped in purple is used for the wings, then the purple dots are added. The veins and cross-markings are also in purple. This butterfly is used in Chapter 9 Fig. 8 (p. 47).

Fig. 10 For a side view of a hovering butterfly proceed as if doing the outline as demonstrated, but add wings on only one side of the body.

Fig. 11 Add a second front wing on the same side as the other wing, slightly above and behind it.

Fig. 10

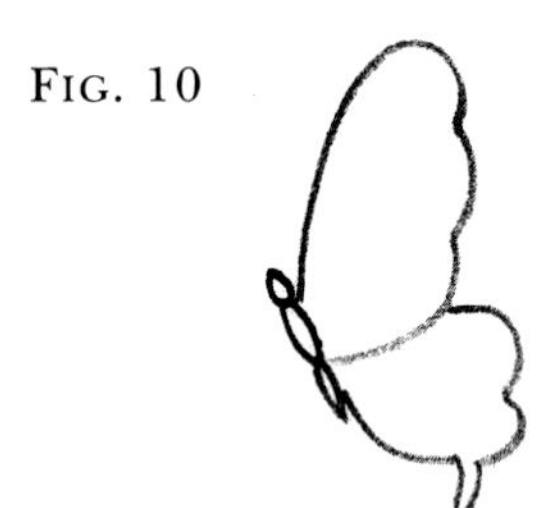

Fig. 11

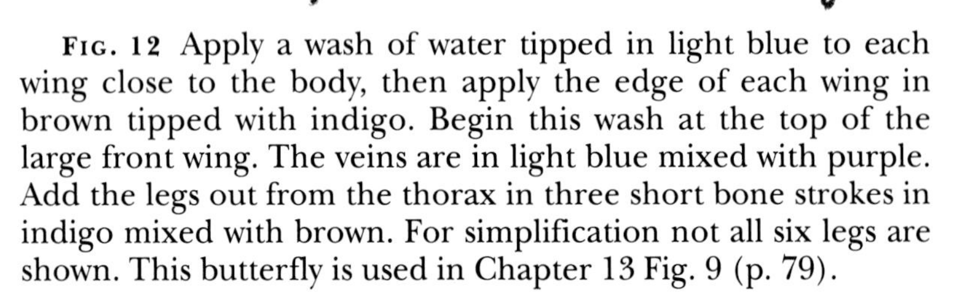

Fig. 12 Apply a wash of water tipped in light blue to each wing close to the body, then apply the edge of each wing in brown tipped with indigo. Begin this wash at the top of the large front wing. The veins are in light blue mixed with purple. Add the legs out from the thorax in three short bone strokes in indigo mixed with brown. For simplification not all six legs are shown. This butterfly is used in Chapter 13 Fig. 9 (p. 79).

CHAPTER 12

ROSES

The examples in this chapter show variations of different styles and a wide range of techniques to depict various qualities of the rose. They can be used to interpret any subject.

In all the styles, no matter how different their outward appearance, they retain the essential qualities of technique that distinguish Chinese painting: variation of line in single strokes and the use of double loaded colour.

The outlining of a subject can be used to explore the complexities of form of an involved subject, from which a simplified brush style painting can be derived.

Before beginning with an outline composition, practise the various qualities of line necessary to depict the characteristics of each of the compositional elements.

Refer to Fig. 5 for the completed outline.

Use a fine brush for all of the outline.

FLOWERS

FIG. 1a Load the brush with a light grey tone (black diluted with water), making sure it is not too wet. Paint a fine orchid leaf stroke. This quality of line and tone is used to express the delicacy of all flower petals.

FIG. 1b Construct a folded inner rose petal in two strokes, from the base of the petal out to the tip.

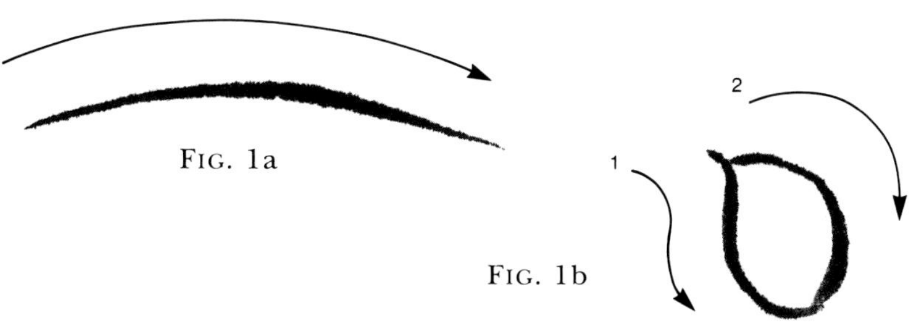

FIG. 1a

FIG. 1b

Leaves

Fig. 2a Load the brush with wet dark ink. Paint a fine needle stroke similar to that for a pine needle. This stroke is used to depict the flexible quality of leaves.

Fig. 2b Construct a rose leaf in three strokes, from the base of the leaf to the tip, the left side, then the right side, then the central vein. Otherwise, form a symmetrical leaf by beginning with the central vein and form the side ones around it.

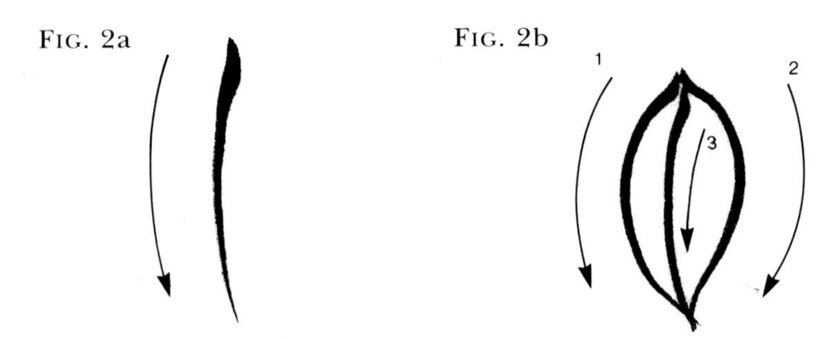

Fig. 2a Fig. 2b

Stems

Fig. 3a Use wet dark ink to paint a fine bone stroke as taut as stretched wire. This has the quality of strength with pliability.

Fig. 3b Outline a stem in two parallel strokes from the flower down. Paint the left side first as this can be seen and used as a guide when adding the right side to maintain an even width. Reverse this procedure if you are left handed. In the example leave a gap in the main stem to join on the side stem.

Fig. 3a Fig. 3b

BRANCHES

FIG. 4a After loading the brush with wet black paint, dab the brush on to a cloth to absorb some of the water from the hairs for a dry brush.

Using the brush on a slight angle and painting quickly, skim across the surface of the paper with a bone stroke. A dry stiff line should result for the rough quality of branches.

FIG. 4b Construct the branch in a series of short connected bone strokes from the stem down, pausing briefly on the paper between each stroke in a jerky rhythm. The branch can be slightly wider towards its base to give the appearance of greater age and strength. Add in the texture markings in dots to indicate knot holes.

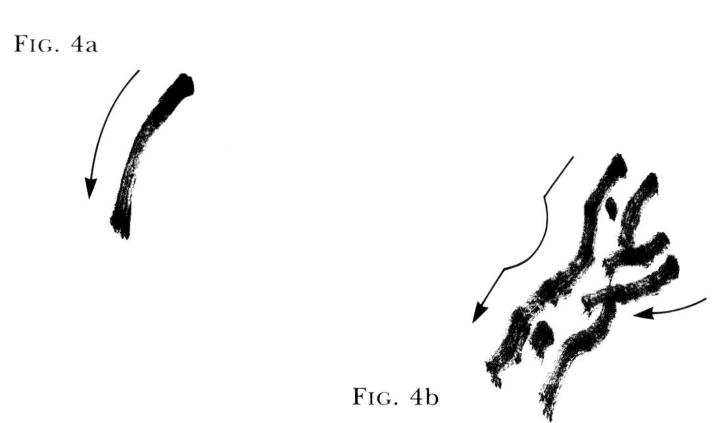

FIG. 4a

FIG. 4b

FIG. 5 A complete outline, referred to as the bone.

Begin with the three inner petals of the flower then add a second layer of four wider petals, each in a single stroke. Both these layers are painted from the base of the petals. Then add the six outer petals in two strokes from their tip to their base.

Next add the buds, also in a light grey, and then the leaves around the flower. Add the calyxes of the flower and the buds in dark ink. Add the nodules below the buds before all the stems, then the small unformed leaves growing from the top of the stems, and the branch and thorns. Finally add the three groups of leaves in the bottom of the composition. For each of these groups first paint a fine bone stroke for the central stem of the group, then attach the leaves to this.

Fig. 5

FIG. 6a Use a white-haired brush for applying the colour wash (referred to as the flesh) and make sure each area has two colours on it. If any area is of only one colour it will appear dull and lifeless, like a flat note in a piece of music. Complete the colour wash on each area in one movement of the brush to avoid a patchy effect.

Fig. 6b This shows the continuous colouring movement, with the tip pointed in the same direction throughout. Move quickly to avoid the paint spreading over the outline. With practise, control of the wash can be quite precise.

First colour the flower with the brush loaded with water, then yellow, and tipped in red. Begin with the centre petals. For each petal keep the tip of the brush pointed towards the centre of the flower so that the red is at the base of the petal: this helps to produce the effect of overlapping petals.

Retip the brush in red before colouring each petal, but there should be enough yellow on the brush to last for the whole flower. The proportions of yellow and red on the brush will depend on the size of the area that is being coloured. After the single movement of the brush has coloured most of the area, it is acceptable to go back and fill in any white spaces left. Use the tip of the brush for this for fine control.

After colouring the flower and the buds, colour the leaves. Use a wash of sap green tipped in indigo. Use this colour also for the calyx of the flower. **Black is not used in any of the colouring as there is enough in the outline**. For the young leaves, the stem, and the calyxes of the buds use sap green tipped in red.

The branch is in a wash of burnt sienna mixed with indigo, tipped in more indigo. The thorns are in red.

Having added the colour, add the details. These are like the features of a person that enliven the subject and give it its individual character.

Fig. 7 With a fine brush add the veins to shape the leaves. Use indigo for the older leaves, red for the younger leaves. The small unformed leaves show no veins yet. Paint over the centre line of the leaf before adding slightly thinner side veins.

Outline the flower and buds in a red-orange colour. Place white spots on to the centre of the flower for the pollen, then overlay them with purple. These are the eyes of the flower and will face it in a given direction.

Refer to Fig. 20 (p. 69) for a brush style rendition of the previous composition. It is a simplification made by extraction of the non-essentials, concerned with the mood of the artist as expressed through the essence of the subject.

First paint the flower. Use a white-haired brush loaded with water then yellow and tipped in red. After a few strokes the brush will need to be retipped in red, but not so much is added for the outer petals as for those in the centre.

Fig. 8 Begin with a teardrop stroke, a shorter version of the example in Chapter 4 Fig. 15 (p. 17).

Fig. 9 Construct the centre of the rose with three folded petals. Each is a separate stroke but placed tightly together. Keep the tip of the brush to the left.

Fig. 8

Fig. 9

Fig. 10 For the next layer of petals, place the brush on the paper with its tip pointed to the centre of the flower, the middle of the three inner petals. Move the brush along from left to right in a series of connected teardrop strokes that become a continuous wriggling motion.

Fig. 11 Add two other petals in a similar manner. Not placing them completely around the centre will help to face the flower in a certain direction, in this case upwards.

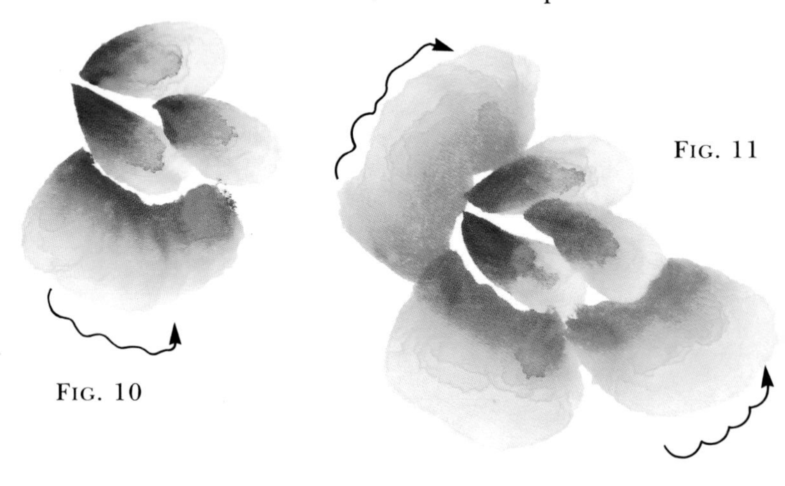

Fig. 11

Fig. 10

Fig. 12 The petals that form the outer layer are completed with two strokes each. Start at the tip of each petal, with the tip of the brush pointed away from the centre of the flower, and paint an orchid leaf stroke in towards the centre. Chapter 4 Fig. 22a (p. 20) describes such a stroke, but the one for the rose is shorter and more curved. Add a second stroke also from the tip of the petal, but away from the first, so that the base of the petal is spread around a petal of the previous layer. Chapter 4 Fig. 22b (p. 20) shows a similar shape, except that for the rose the two strokes do not come together at their finish but are spread apart.

Fig. 13 Add the other outer petals to the flower. Make sure each one has the characteristic pointed rose petal shape. Add the sepals with a red-haired brush loaded with sap green and tipped in indigo, using a short sharp needle stroke. The stems are painted with a red-haired brush loaded with sap green tipped with red using a bone stroke.

FIG. 14 Construct the bud in two short teardrop strokes, from the tip down. The proportions of yellow and red are about even.

FIG. 15 With a red-haired brush, loaded with sap green and tipped in red, add a calyx using orchid leaf strokes, then add a round nodule below the bud. Use a fine bone stroke for the stem of the bud. The leaves on the stem are in an orchid leaf stroke. All these strokes are painted downwards.

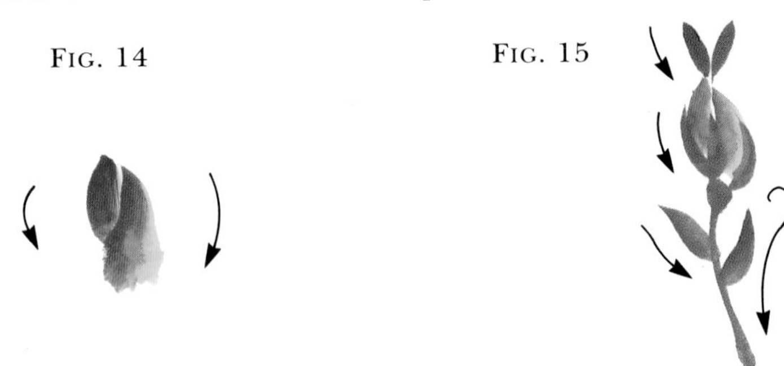
FIG. 14 FIG. 15

FIG. 16 Use a red-haired brush loaded with sap green tipped in black to paint a bone stroke to form the central stem of a leaf group.

FIG. 17 With the same loaded brush, add each leaf in two short orchid leaf strokes from the base to the tip to form a short, rounded leaf.

FIG. 16 FIG. 17

FIG. 18 A typical leaf group for roses is a pattern of five. Make sure each leaf is attached to the stem.

FIG. 19 For the thorns use a fine brush loaded with red to paint a short, sharp needle stroke in a vigorous upward movement that then curves down at its point.

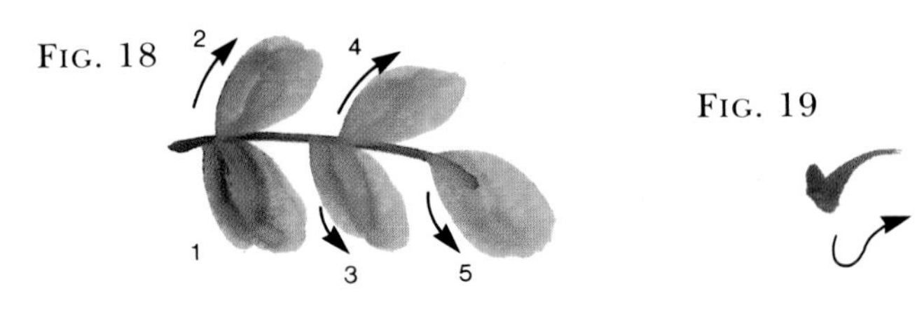

FIG. 18 FIG. 19

Fig. 20 The completed composition. Illustrating how to transform a line drawing, Fig. 7, into a brush style painting.

Paint the flower, then the buds, then the leaves around the flower, then the calyxes, stems and unformed leaves. The branch is then added, in burnt sienna tipped in black, then the

lower leaf group and the thorns. The stamens of the flower are placed directly into the centre in a reddish purple.

Fig. 21 A traditional rendition of a white flower. There is no white paint actually used, as it was not a colour available to the traditional palette, being a pigment not found in China.

Fig. 22

Later, when white paint was introduced from the west, it was incorporated as shown in Chapter 16. However, the more traditional method on white paper is still used and is favoured.

Outline the flower in a pale blue with a fine brush. Its construction is as for the flower in Fig. 5 (p. 61) but the lines are slightly thicker. Add a colour wash to the lower half of each petal and bud with a white-haired brush loaded with water and tipped in a light blue. Keep the tip of the brush pointed towards the centre of the flower, to form a shading to each petal. Retip the brush for each petal. This is a similar technique to doing the wash for the wings of the butterflies, especially as in Chapter 11 Fig. 5 (p. 56). Blue is used for the outline and the wash as it is the colour that is most usually reflected by a white surface as traditionally understood by the Chinese artist.

The rest of the painting is then carried out as for the previous example. The older leaves are in sap green tipped in indigo, in keeping with the softer tones of the flower. A basic principle for all flowers is that the lighter the flower the lighter the leaves appear, and conversely the darker the flower the darker the leaves appear, as in the next example where this has been taken to its extreme.

Fig. 22 This is a further extraction towards the essence. The colour is removed from all the supporting features so as not to distract from the vitality of the flower, which is coloured in the most vital of colours, red. This is a method much used in *Sumi-é*, Japanese ink painting, where often the colour is extracted from the flower as well. The many tones of black contain all colours, just as white reflects all colours.

All the brush strokes used are as in the example in Fig. 20. For the flower use a white-haired brush loaded with water then rose madder, and tipped in alizarin crimson. The leaves are in light grey tipped in black. Tip the brush in less black for the stems and smaller leaves. A dry stroke is used for the branch and pure black for the calyxes, thorns and stamens.

CHAPTER 13

THE SEVEN GREENS

Leaves are important in their supporting role: with their deep tones of blues and greens which enhance the high tones of the yellows and the reds of the flowers; for their placement in the composition helping to lift the flower up and push it forward, and for their use as a mass of deep tones to balance the empty spaces. They are also significant for their own particular grace and beauty, derived from their glossiness and flexibility, their abundance and lasting quality.

To emphasize the individual character of leaves—not having the bright colours available to the flowers—there has evolved, in traditional Chinese painting, a grading of seven mixtures of colour to portray different ages of leaves and to give each leaf its unique position among the order of nature. For even among something as plain as leaves, no two are the same.

While not all the seven mixtures contain green, they all contain that quality which is the essence of foliage: calm depth.

The following examples not only display the seven greens but also form interesting leaf patterns in themselves. This is always a worthwhile study, as usually we are not so observant of leaves as we are of their brighter partners, flowers. The younger more colourful leaves are more pointed. The older, deeper-toned leaves are more rounded. All are made of two strokes, from the base to the tip, except for the young leaves in Fig. 4 which are painted from the tip down. The second named colour is on the tip of the brush. Each group is painted with the one load of the brush. Start with the centre foremost leaf in each group then add the other leaves, alternating left then right towards the outside and back of the front row of leaves, then add those leaves beneath this first group. Only one leaf in each group has been veined, in the second named colour, as an example.

The first four groups become progressively younger.

FIG. 1 Green and black.

FIG. 2 Green and dark blue (indigo).

FIG. 3 Green and brown (burnt sienna).

FIG. 4 Green and red.

The next three groups become progressively older.

FIG. 5 Brown and dark blue.
FIG. 6 Brown and black.
FIG. 7 Dark blue and black.

FIG. 5

FIG. 6

FIG. 7

The following two compositions incorporate most of the above greens.

BIRD AND ROSES

FIG. 8a Do not be daunted by the apparent complexity of this, our first involved composition. Visualise the painting in three sections with a rose in each, no more difficult than previously attempted. A lot of Chinese painting is repetition of basic patterns in endless variations. If, when painting, the elements in the composition become too many just leave some out in the first attempts until everything can be placed in proportion.

BIRD

This is the host: according to its size, position in the composition and by its potential activity (yang). Paint the bird

FIG. 8a

first, as described in Chapter 18 Fig. 7 (p. 120). Even if the first painted bird is not too successful as long as it has some resemblance to a bird it will be useful. Then add the other elements to practise the full arrangement of the composition. Don't wait until you have painted a respectable bird then spoil the painting in some other aspect because these parts have not been practised. About four to six practise birds should solve most of the difficulties, the main one being proportion. When painting the bird leave a lot of space around it, especially in front, so that the bird can easily fly away. Its colour reflects the leaves, there is no competition with the flowers: each has its own place in the harmony of nature.

FLOWERS

These are the guests. Paint the full-open flower below the bird then the side-on flower to its right, the small just-opening flower which the bird is greeting. Finally, add the buds.

LEAVES

Paint the darkest group first—the blue and black—then the brown and black, then the green and black, then the green and blue, then the young (green and red) leaves. The small groups of leaves, directly attached to the branches, are not painted until the branch has been added.

After the large leaves add the calyxes and stems, then add the unformed leaves placing them off the stems; all painted in sap green tipped in red.

BRANCH

In burnt sienna tipped in black, begin with the longest branch, working down from the top, behind the bird and the large rose. Make sure that the branch is placed firmly between the feet of the bird, so that it has a good grip.

FIG. 8b

After adding the small leaf groups, each leaf in one brush stroke, add the veins to all the leaves in the appropriate colours, then the thorns and the moss dots.

If there is difficulty in the placement of any of the compositional elements then study the white spaces between the elements for a deeper understanding of their positions.

The calligraphy is added last and reads 'flower and bird'. Follow the brush stroke order as shown in Fig 8b.

POPPIES AND BUTTERFLY

FIG. 9 A bunch of poppies in various, joyous colours, dancing in an early morning breeze.

FLOWERS

They are the hosts: the red one is painted with water tipped in rose madder, then the purple one is tipped in red, and next the yellow one is also tipped in red. Add the same coloured bud as each flower is painted. Add the white flower using the same technique as for the white rose in Chapter 12 Fig. 21 (p. 70). When each flower is dry, add the veins. The veins are in the darkest colour on that particular flower.

Add the unopened buds, calyxes and stems in sap green tipped in indigo. The formation of the stems is a special feature of this composition. Use a very upright brush but not too stiff a line to form the intersections of the white spaces.

LEAVES

These leaves are more segmented than those shown in Chapter 8. Paint the blue and black leaves first, then the green and black leaves, then the green and blue leaves, then the green and red leaves. The leaves have veins in a mixture of white and sap green; the veins of the green and red leaves have red added to this mixture. Add a light green centre of sap green tipped in a light blue to each flower.

Place white for the stamens then overlay with yellow. Short, fine needle strokes are used for the bristles on the calyxes and the top of the stems.

BUTTERFLY

The guest, just arrived, is about to alight on a flower: which one will it choose? This butterfly is described in Chapter 11 Fig 12 (p.58).

FIG. 9

CHAPTER 14

蓮 *LOTUS*

The lotus and the peony are the two most exalted and the two most difficult flowers to paint.

The lotus is associated with the religious symbol of Buddhism, revered for the purity of the colours of its firm petals and its exquisite fragrance, held aloft out of the mud of the lake in which its stems are rooted. Thus a person can retain their integrity and be pure of heart even among the mundane existence of everyday life.

Refer to Fig. 11 for the completed composition.

FIG. 1 Begin with the flower, with the petal at the centre closest to the front. Use a red-haired brush, loaded with water then rose madder, tipped in purple. Paint an orchid leaf stroke from the tip of the petal to its base.

FIG. 2 Place a second similar stroke next to this to form one petal. This technique is described in more detail in Chapter 4 Figs. 22a and 22b (p. 20).

FIG. 1

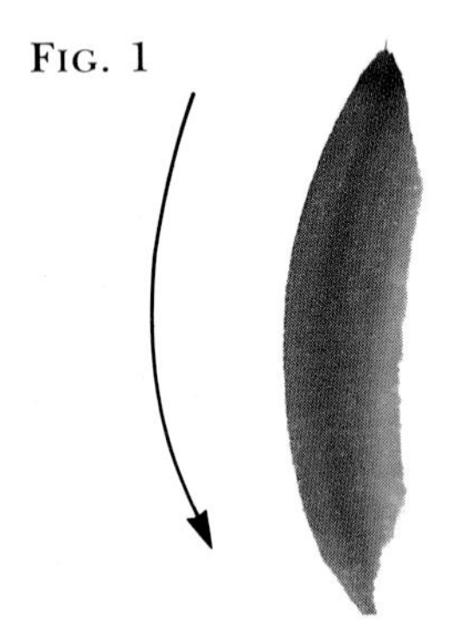

FIG. 2

FIG. 3 Add the other petals, each with two strokes, placing those in the front on either side of the first petal in the order shown. When beginning each petal retip the brush in purple.

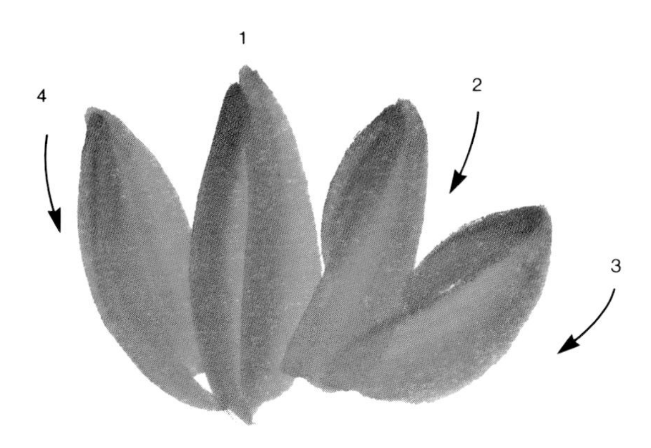

FIG. 4 Add two short petals as if they are behind the front ones. Do not retip the brush for these and they will appear lighter and thus seem to be set behind the others.

FIG. 5 When the flower is dry, use a fine brush loaded with purple toned with black to paint short, sharp needle strokes in the centre of the flower for the stamens.

FIG. 5

FIG. 4

FIG. 6 Next add the leaves. While the flower is big, as large as two cupped hands, the leaves are bigger, large enough to hold a baby, as was said of the baby Buddha who was found in the petals of a lotus flower. Begin with the centre of the leaf. Use a white-haired brush, loaded with sap green and tipped in black to paint a dot, with the tip of the brush pointed to the left. This acts as a focal point for the other strokes and makes it easier to form the shape of the leaf.

FIG. 7 Recharge the brush. Load it well with sap green tipped in plenty of black, and use the brush on a low angle to paint a series of bone strokes of graduated length and tone out from the centre of the leaf. Add the strokes left to right across the front of the leaf.

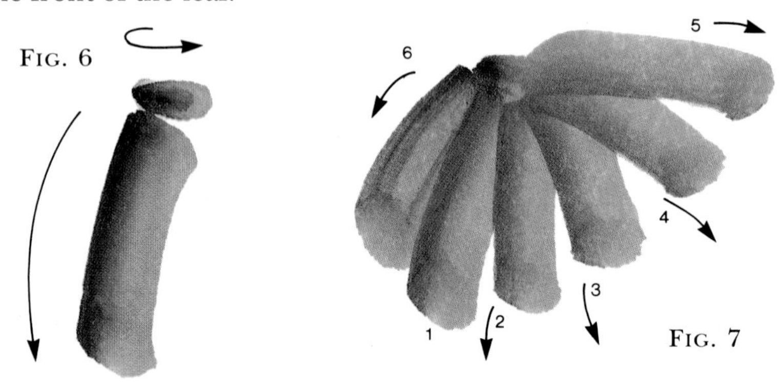

FIG. 6

FIG. 7

FIG. 8 Complete the leaf with shorter bone strokes along the back of the leaf. This technique is fully explained in Chapter 4 Fig. 8 (p. 14).

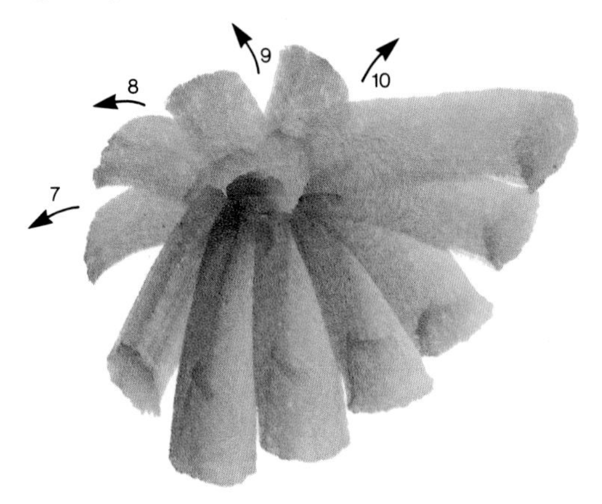

Fig. 9 With an upright red-haired brush loaded with sap green and tipped in indigo, paint a long thin bone stroke for each stem from the base of the flower or leaf downward. Make it only slightly bent, and strong enough to hold up its large burden.

Fig. 10 Add soft thorns with a downward dot in black, alternating left then right down the stem.

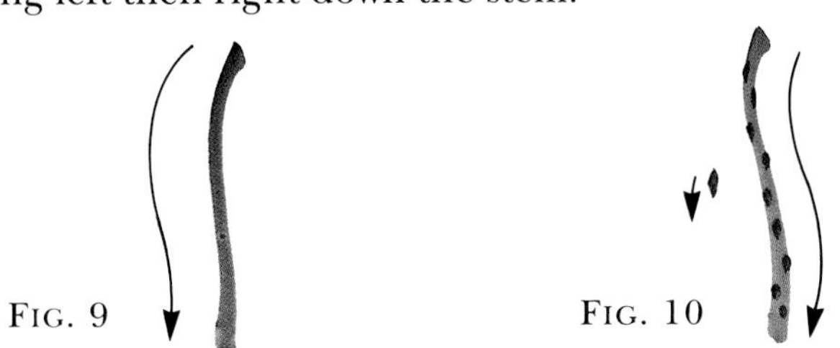

Fig. 9 Fig. 10

Fig. 11 The completed composition.

First paint the flower then the leaf then the stems. Paint the leaf stem first as it is darker than the flower stem. Slightly retip

the brush in indigo for the flower stem, then add the thorns to the stems and the stamens to the flower.
In the more complex composition of Fig. 16 there appears additional elements as explained below.

Fig. 12 The young folded leaf is painted with a white-haired brush loaded with sap green tipped in red, with a series of short, wide bone strokes painted downwards.

Fig. 13 Add the other strokes for the underneath of the leaf from left to right, working from the first stroke.

Fig. 14 Add the top of the young leaf in another series of bone strokes, from left to right, curved so as to form an oyster-shell like shape. Retip the brush in red as necessary.

The veins are added when the flower and the leaves are dry, using a fine brush and thin needle strokes.

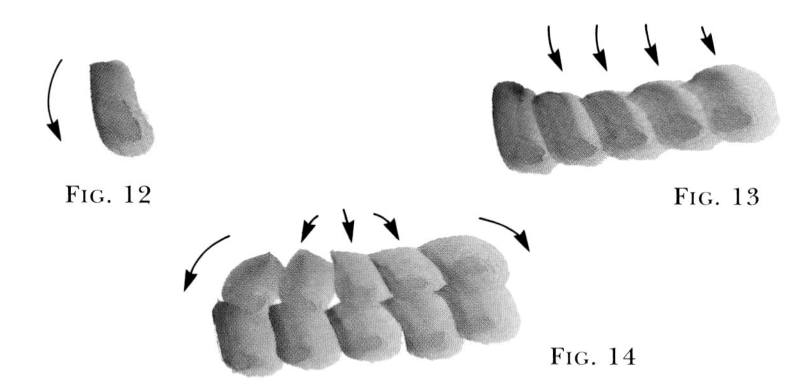
Fig. 12 Fig. 13 Fig. 14

Fig. 15a Use a reddish orange for the flower veins: they extend about halfway up each petal and are only on the outsides of the petals.

Fig. 15b An example leaf vein in sap green tipped in indigo. Paint the central vein before adding the side veins.

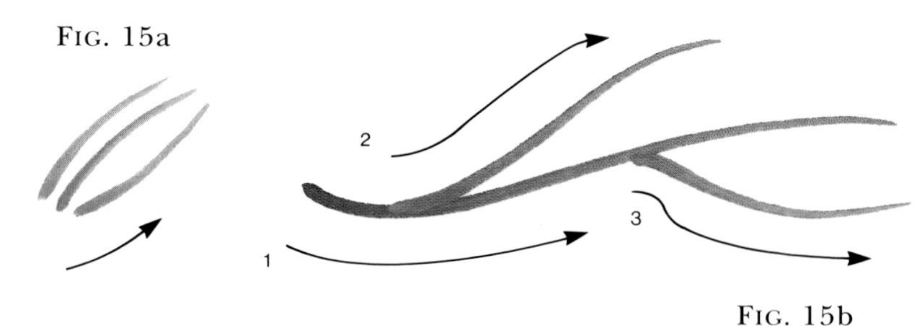

Fig. 15a Fig. 15b

Fig. 16

FIG. 16 A complex composition.

FLOWERS

Use yellow tipped in red for the flowers. First paint the bud then the flower below and to its left, and then the bottom right flower.

LEAVES

The large one is in sap green and black, then paint the sap green and indigo leaf, then the young one.

CALYXES

In sap green tipped in indigo, using a short teardrop stroke.

STEM

Form irregular but interesting white areas with the intersection of stems, leaves and flowers. Check that each flower and leaf has been given a stem and that if a stem goes behind a flower or leaf it also reappears below it and follows in a natural line.

Add the details of thorns, stamens and veins. The leaf veins are in the appropriate colour for each leaf. Begin the veins of the large leaf by outlining the centre and a cross central line using fine bone strokes. The veins are added with a stroke out from the centre of the leaf almost to its edge. Every second vein has side veins extending from it. The veins for the young leaf help to form its closed appearance.

CHAPTER 15

FISH

Begin with some basic fish to learn the technique before placing them in compositions.

FIG. 1 With a red-haired brush loaded with sap green and tipped in light blue, paint a long needle stroke to form the back of the body, as described in Chapter 4 Fig. 10 (p. 15).

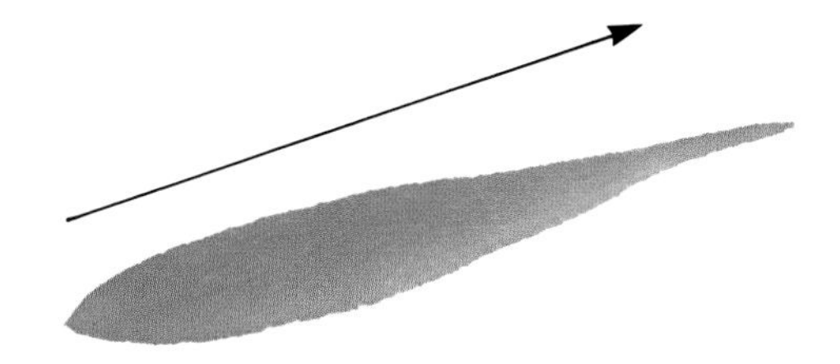

FIG. 2 Add two shorter needle strokes for the tail.

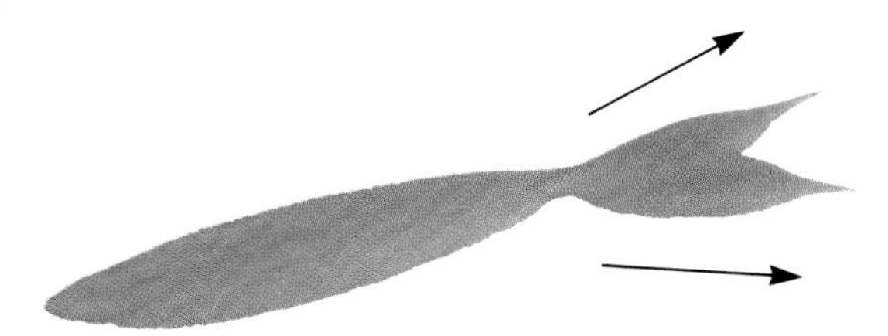

FIG. 3 Add a fine line for the underneath of the body. The slight indentation just after the start of the line forms the head.

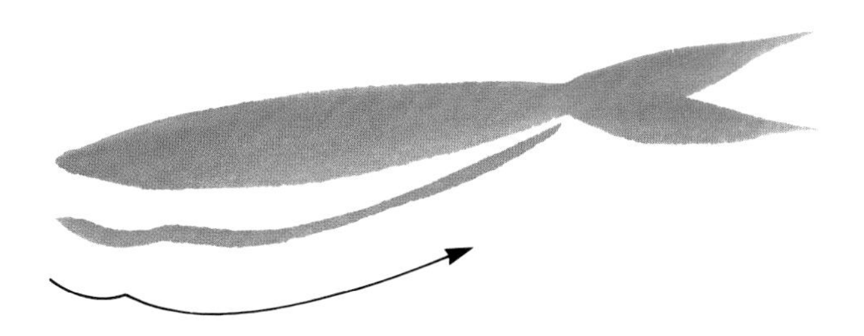

Fig.4 Use short teardrop strokes for the gills and fins, painting them out from the body.

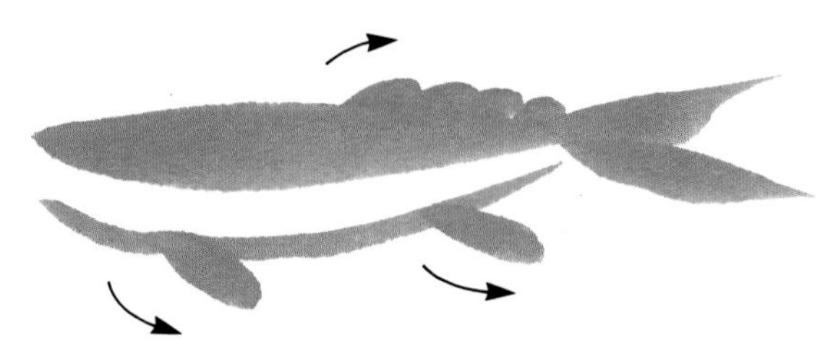

Fig. 5 With a fine brush loaded with red, add two dots for the eyes and two curved bone strokes for the mouth.

WILLOW AND FISH Fig. 6

Fish

Do all the bodies then the tails then the details.

Willow

As for a stem of wisteria leaves. Use a longer stem and add more leaves, which are painted towards the stem in sap green tipped in indigo, from the tip of the stem to the top of the paper. Place two leaves on the water to attract the fish.

Water

Add the lines with a fine brush loaded with light blue mixed with a small amount of indigo, using a fine orchid line as described in Chapter 4 Fig. 25a (p. 22). Do not add too many water lines, they are only a suggestion. Place some over the bodies of the fish to sit them beneath the water.

Fig. 6

Fig. 7 With a red-haired brush loaded with light blue tipped in purple, paint a short needle stroke for the body of a small fish as described in Chapter 4 Fig. 11b (p. 16).

Fig. 8 Add two short needle strokes from the rear of the body to form the tail.

Fig. 9 Complete this fish as for the previous one, but give it a rounder mouth.

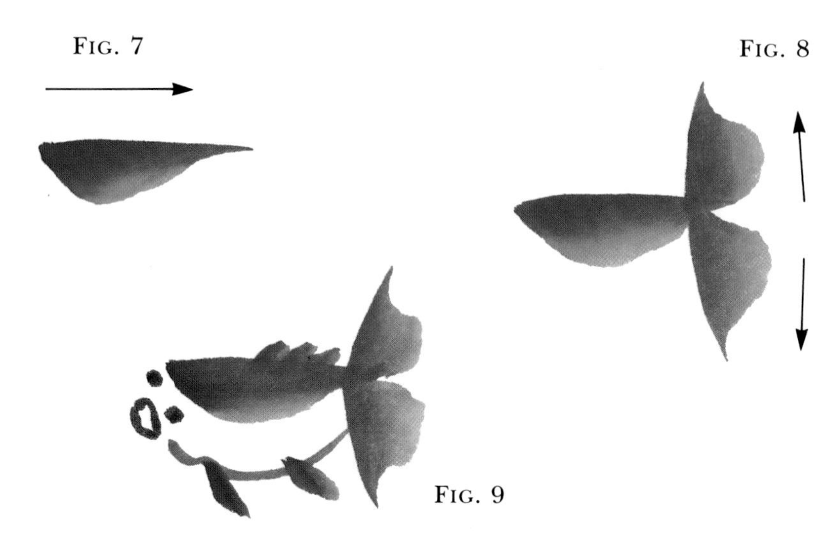

Fig. 7

Fig. 8

Fig. 9

Fig. 10 Use a red-haired brush loaded with sap green tipped in indigo to depict seaweed, with an elongated teardrop stroke.

Fig. 11 A completed group. Each leaf is painted from the tip to its base, as described in Chapter 4 Fig. 19 (p. 19).

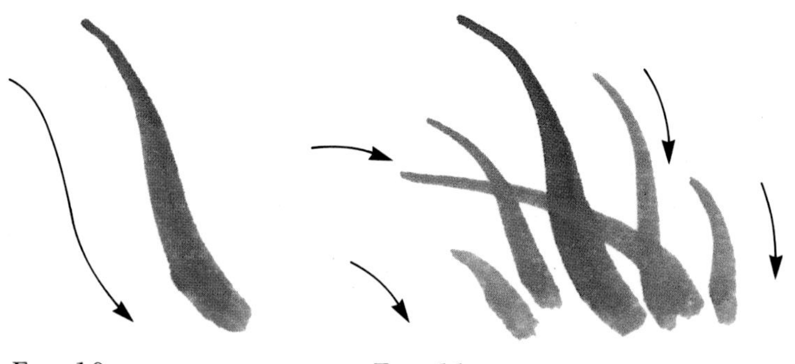

Fig. 10

Fig. 11

Fig. 12 Begin with all the bodies then the tails, then all of the detail. Add the seaweed, then the undulating water pattern in a light blue mixed with indigo, using a fine orchid leaf stroke. The fish, seaweed and water use repetition to express harmony.

GOLDFISH

Fig.13 Construct the main body stroke as for the fish in Fig. 1 but with the brush at a lower angle for a thicker stroke and loaded with yellow tipped in red.

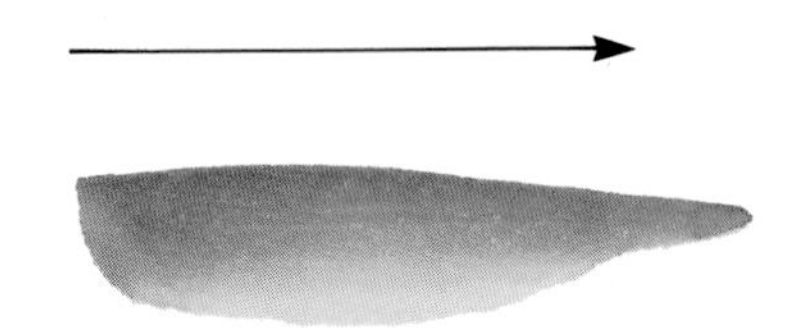

Fig. 14 Begin the tail with an elongated teardrop stroke as described in Chapter 4 Fig.16 (p. 18).

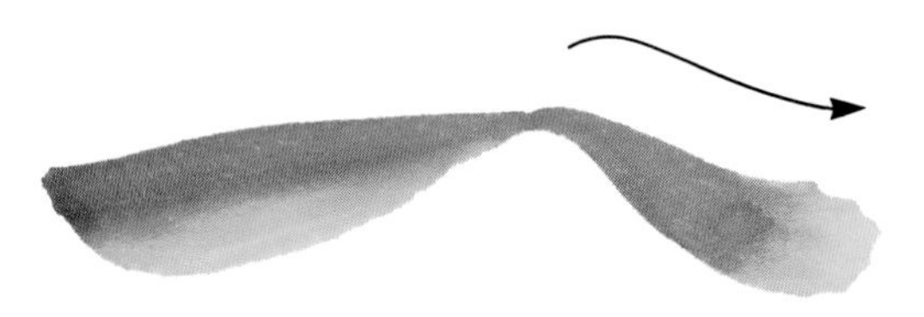

Fig. 15 Complete the tail in four strokes.

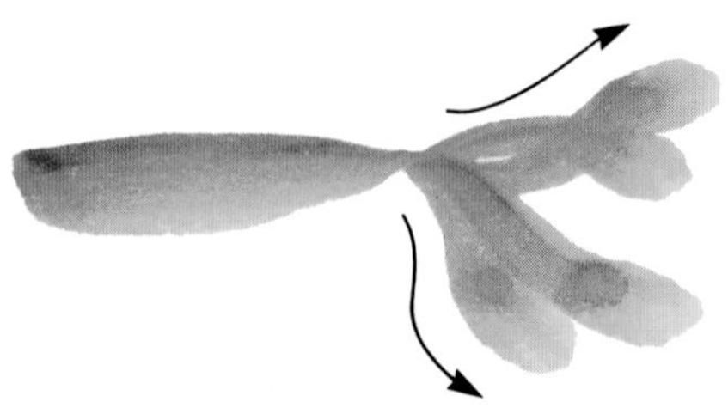

Fig. 16 Retip the brush in red and add a series of short teardrop strokes along the inside of the body stroke to round off the body and to widen it.

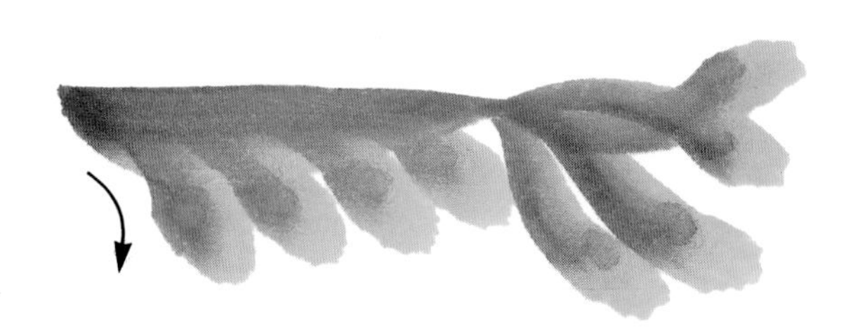

Fig. 17 Add the underside of the body, the fins and the face, as for the other fish. Use black for the face features.

LOTUS AND GOLDFISH Fig. 18

Flowers
The flowers and the buds are in rose madder tipped in purple.

Leaves
They are in their various greens. Then add the stems and all the details. For the stamens lay down white and overlay with yellow when it is dry.

Add the fish in quiet conversation and finally the gently moving water lines.

CHAPTER 16

WHITE FLOWERS ON COLOURED RICE PAPER

白花

Traditionally, white flowers were depicted in an outline of soft blue with or without a pale wash on the lower half of the petals, as in the example in Chapter 12 Fig. 21 (p. 70). This is in keeping with the concept of using the minimum to convey the maximum by allowing the existing white (of the paper) to be used as its own colour. Since the introduction of white paint, and when realism is needed, white paint is accepted.

Most watercolour white is very translucent, designed to use to mix with a colour to produce a lighter tone of that colour (tinting)—for instance red and white to make pink, or black and white to make grey—whereas water is used in this way in Chinese painting, for example red and water is used to make pink. Because of the translucency of the better quality whites, including the misnamed 'Chinese white', they are not suitable where white is needed as a colour in itself. A more opaque white is required. Some tubes in sets of watercolours are thicker bodied, made of coarser pigment. If there is difficulty in obtaining an opaque watercolour white use a poster colour or even a tempera white.

Before proceeding with the painting it is necessary to give a colour wash to the rice paper for a contrasting background. Alternatively, a naturally dark tone of paper such as mulberry paper can be used, or coloured silk (mounting techniques are explained in Chapter 17).

COLOUR WASH

Use a 2.5 or 5 cm house painting brush with soft hair so as not to tear the rice paper. In a wide, shallow container—such as an empty margarine tub—add two parts indigo to one part brown paint. The amount needed will depend on the size of the rice paper to be coloured, its thickness, absorbency and the strength of tone required.

Add about a teaspoon of water to the paint and mix them together using the brush until all the paint is dissolved. Add more water as needed to bring the wash to its desired strength. Test it on a small piece of rice paper. Make sure there is enough wash as rice paper will absorb a lot.

Lay down some backing paper to absorb the excess wash that might soak through the rice paper (use newspaper or butcher's paper). Lay a sheet of rice paper on top of this, either side facing up.

Charge the brush well with wash and begin at the bottom of the paper, applying the wash in single, horizontal strokes, that slightly overlap each other to avoid streaking. Reload the brush after each stroke to keep an even tone. Alternatively, keep painting with the one brush load for a diminishing, faded effect as the brush runs out of wash. The examples in this chapter are of flat, even washes.

When the rice paper is covered with the wash remove it from the backing paper—it will be very fragile—and lay it on some clean, dry paper. After about five minutes transfer it to another sheet to completely dry before painting on it. Colour a number of sheets at the one session for later use.

The painting in Fig. 1 is on rice paper coloured in the above proportions of indigo and brown. The rice paper used in Figs. 2 and 3 has been coloured with a mixture of two parts brown to one part indigo.

Most background colours can be used as long as the tone is deep enough for the white to stand out. Some coloured flowers can look effective on a light toned wash. Traditionally the more neutral tones are preferred as they do not compete with the colours in the painting.

White is only used for flowers, butterflies, or birds and then only as itself not to tint colours and never to tone leaves, stems, or branches as it would inappropriately soften their character.

Begin each painting by applying the white. First apply a flat coat as undercoat. Allow this to completely dry before applying the second coat of white that has been tipped in the correct colour.

ROSES Fig. 1

Flowers
After the white undercoat of the flowers and buds is dry add a second coat of white with the brush tipped in yellow mixed with red. Use the same strokes as for the rose in Chapter 12 Fig. 20 (p. 69).

Leaves
Leaves are in green tipped in black and green tipped in red; blue in the leaves would be inappropriate here as there is enough blue in the background. Add calyxes and stems then the unformed leaves on the stems and the leaf veins. The stamens are in red mixed with purple.

HIBISCUS Fig. 2

This is a brush style painting of the outline version in Chapter 17 Fig. 15 (p. 111).

Flowers
Paint a white undercoat with the technique described in Chapter 4 Fig. 17 (p. 18). Add a second coat with white tipped in a light blue. Keep the tip of the brush pointed towards the centre of the flower. It is a five petalled flower.

Leaves
Added with the same technique as for the hydrangea leaves or as described in Chapter 4 Fig. 12b (p. 16). Each leaf is of three sections: the middle section is the widest and longest and is painted first, then the sections, one on either side, are added. The older leaves are in sap green tipped in indigo. The younger leaves are in sap green tipped in red. Brown would be inappropriate as there is enough in the background wash.

FIG. 1

After the leaves, add the calyx around the bud in sap green tipped in indigo, then add the stems and the two unformed leaves off the stem in sap green tipped in red.

Veins

Add when the flowers and the leaves are almost dry, in a light blue mixed with a little purple for the flowers. For each petal the central vein is the longest. The side veins diminish in length to the edge of the petal. They are all curved to give depth to the flower and do not reach the edge of the petal. For the veins on the older leaves use a mixture of sap green, yellow and white. Add red to this mixture for the veins on the young leaves.

The pistil and pollen dots are in red mixed with purple.

Butterfly

As described in Chapter 11 Fig. 9 (p. 58), except that white is laid on the wings before a second coat of white tipped in yellow is added. Add the wing markings and the outline in yellow mixed with a little red. The eyes and antennae are in red mixed with purple.

BIRD AND POPPY Fig. 3

Bird and Buds

Outline in pale ink as described in Chapter 19 Fig. 6 (p. 132). Give the bird an undercoat of white inside the outline, and an undercoat of white to the buds. Add a second coat of plain white to the bird to strengthen it and a second coat of white tipped with light blue for the buds.

Use a fine brush loaded with a light blue mixed with indigo to re-outline and add the details of the bird's body, wings and tail. Use black to outline the beak and the eye, then fill these in with yellow. Use pale red for the legs and black for the claws. Add light blue to the inside edges of the wings and tail and around the face markings and then blend it into the white with a brush dampened with a little water. Use light blue for the veins of the poppy buds.

Finish the rest of the poppy as in Chapter 8 Fig. 8 (p 41). Use sap green tipped in indigo for the darker leaves. Finally add the grass in fine teardrop strokes—similar to the seaweed in Chapter 15 Fig. 10 (p. 90), but shorter and less curved—and paint the grass from tips to the ground in sap green tipped in black. The horizontal lines of grass help to anchor the bird on the ground.

FIG. 2

FIG. 3

CHAPTER 17
PAINTING ON SILK

Silk was used as a painting surface before the invention of paper. Mainly landscapes were painted, in the outline method with soft colour washes. With the advent of paper, with its greater absorbency, the quicker one-brush-stroke style was developed to cope with it: as flower painting became more popular it was usually executed in this method. Rice paper was also sized to make it suitable for the outline style.

Silk can be used for the one stroke style, but it is the ideal surface for the outline method because it has some absorbency to take the wash but not so much absorbency as to diffuse the clarity of line. Further, the use of silk and the outline method also evokes the much revered ancient aspects of Chinese brush painting. The surfaces of the old silk paintings have turned from white to brown over the centuries: in imitation of this, silks of this colour are often used. Most soft, neutral colours are suitable as long as the colour does not dominate the painting.

MOUNTING

While rice paper is usually painted on before it is mounted, silk is mounted first to help size it and to prevent it stretching. Traditionally, it was mounted on to thick rice paper for scrolls or screens, but otherwise the best way to preserve the painting on permanent display is to mount it on thick cardboard (to prevent sagging) and to put it in a glass frame. Traditional painting silk, pre-mounted on rice paper, can be purchased from specialised Chinese art shops and elsewhere. Otherwise dress silk can be used or—cheaper and more convenient—even synthetic dress lining can be used. Dress linings come in a wide range of colours, are about a quarter the price of pure silk, are readily available (often as off-cuts from dress making) and require no sizing.

Thick ten-sheet pasteboard from a newsagent, stationer, art supplier or sign writing supplier is an ideal backing board. The larger the piece of silk to be mounted, the thicker the board must be. The board should not buckle when the silk is mounted on it, but if the board just bends slightly it can be flattened when dry. Cut the silk about 2.5 cm wider all around than the board.

Lay the silk, either side down, on a non-absorbent surface, such as a laminated kitchen table top. Cut off any loose strands of silk before applying the glue. With a soft 2.5 or 5 cm wide house painting brush apply a paper glue, such as school paste or PVA, diluted with enough water to make it easy to spread. The thicker the silk the thicker glue needs to be. If when the mounted silk is dry it lifts away from the surface of the board then the glue needs to be thicker. Mount a small piece as practice first.

When applying the glue begin at the centre of the silk and paint in single strokes out towards the edges. Any wrinkles will be smoothed out by the watery glue. When the silk is covered with a layer of glue lay the board on the top of it so that there is a 2.5 cm edge of silk all around. Be sure to place the board in the middle of the piece of silk as it will be difficult to adjust after it has been laid down.

Press the board down firmly, running your hand over the back to ensure each area of silk is stuck to the board.

Starting with one of the longer edges, pick up the overlap of silk and fold it back over the board, pulling it taut before pressing it down, and adding more glue if necessary. Do the same to the other long edge. Make sure you pull each edge taut before gluing it down, as this will remove any slack on the other side. When doing the two shorter edges there will be a doubled thickness of silk at the corners: pleat them into a triangular shape and add more glue before pressing them down. If they are too bulky most of the excess can be cut off, but not too close to the edge of the board.

Turn the board over and lay it on a piece of paper, silk side up, to dry. With a slightly damp sponge wipe off any excess glue from the surface of the silk. The table top will also need to be cleaned and dried before another piece can be mounted.

SIZING

If using a lining it will be ready to use when it is dry. If using pure silk it will need to be sized. Purchase alum from a chemist —this is in the form of small white crystals—dissolve it in an equivalent amount of warm water and apply it to the dried surface of the silk and to the back folded edges. The same brush as for the glueing can be used. After the first coat of size is dry test on the back to gauge the absorbency of the sized silk. Paint some fine strokes with dark wet black: if the line bleeds, that is if there is a fuzzy edge along the weave of the silk, then a second coat of size will be needed. Two coats are usually enough. Don't apply too much size or else it will be difficult for the silk to absorb any paint. After each coat of size is dry some crystals will be left on the surface: brush them off gently so as not to scratch the silk. The folded edge can also be used to see the results of various paint colours on a coloured silk.

This is a fair amount of preparation and the painting is much slower, but the results are well worth the effort.

While the silk is drying practise the following strokes suitable for outline technique. The techniques are extensions of those shown in Chapter 12 Figs. 1–4 (pp. 59–61) and can also be applied to the outlining of the butterflies and the birds.

Each set of strokes is painted with the one brush load of paint, using an upright fine brush in a continuous series of movement that become one. Work from left to right and from top to bottom. The arrows indicate the direction and the first and last stroke.

FIGS. 1 & 2 Soft lines for petals, underneath of birds, butterfly wings. Use an orchid leaf stroke with light grey.

FIG. 1

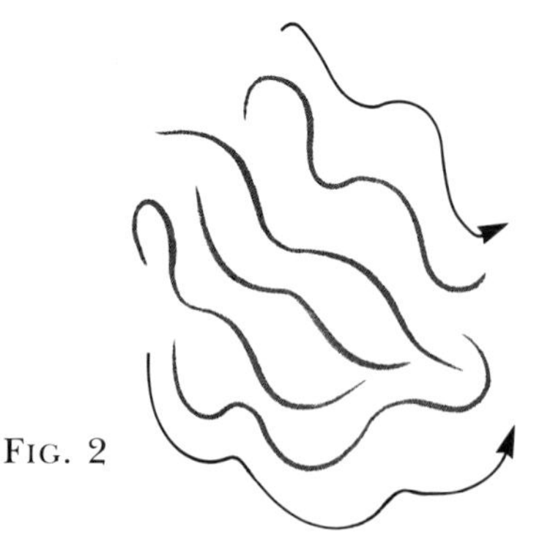

FIG. 2

FIG. 3 Resilient lines for leaves, birds beaks, or flower and leaf veins. Use needle strokes with dark wet black.

FIGS. 4 and 5 Vigorous strokes for leaves and leaf veins, bird wings and tail markings. Use hook strokes with dark wet black.

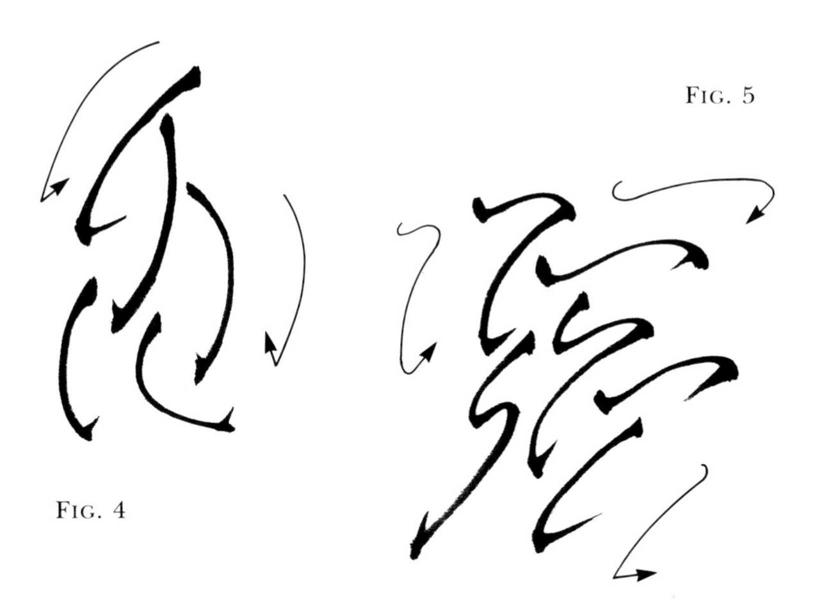

FIG. 4

FIG. 5

FIG. 6 Strong, pliant lines for stems or vines, birds legs, or butterfly bodies. Use bone strokes with dark wet black.

FIG. 7 Strong rough lines for branches. Use bone strokes with dry, dark black. The brush is held on an angle for this stroke and moved quickly for the effect known as 'flying white'.

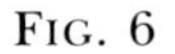

FIG. 6

Before using these strokes to begin a silk painting carefully read *SILK PRINTING PRINCIPLES* on pages 114–15.

FIG. 7

HIBISCUS

Refer to Fig. 15 for the complete composition. The composition is the same as the brush style version in Chapter 16 Fig. 2 (p. 100), the main differences are the colours of the flowers and butterfly.

Fig. 8 Begin with the outline of the flowers in soft, light orchid strokes from the centre of the flower out to the edge, forming a three lobed petal with the middle lobe slightly longer, then back to the centre. Do this in one continuous, smooth stroke. Do not pause. Paint the front petal first then the one to its left, alternating to the rear petal in the order shown.

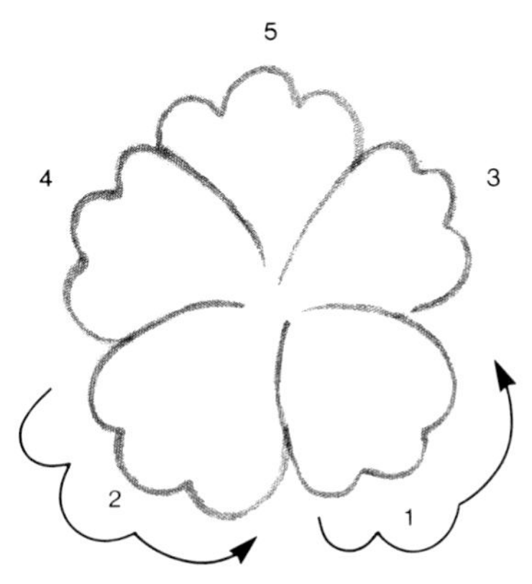

Fig. 9 Add alizarin crimson to the outer areas of each petal.

FIG. 10 Add purple to the central area of each petal and then blend the purple into the red to about one third of the way to the edge, as shown in Fig. 15. Colour each flower separately as that is a large enough area to work on at one time.

When the flowers are dry add a coloured outline in a reddish purple. The veins are also in this colour: they extend at the most only three-quarters of the way out along each petal. Add the pistil and the pollen dots, first in an undercoat of white then in a second coat of white or yellow as appropriate.

FIG. 11 Outline the leaves in three sections. Begin with the central section, with a needle stroke for the vein, then add each side of the leaf, all in dark, wet ink.

FIG. 12 Add the two side sections of the leaf in the order shown, beginning with the centre vein each time. When adding the leaves to the composition place them as close as possible to the flowers so that they appear to come from behind them.

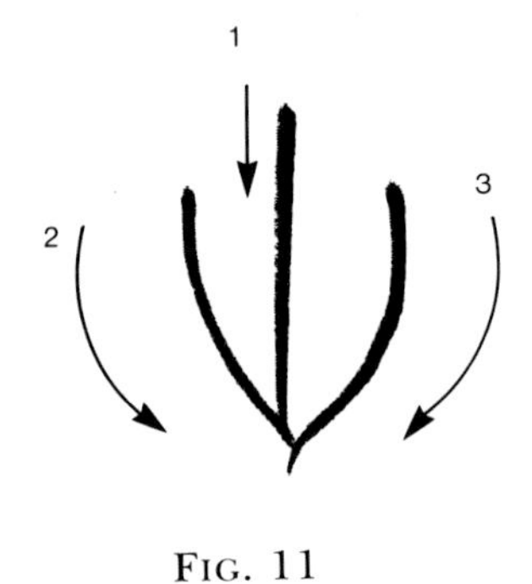

FIG. 11

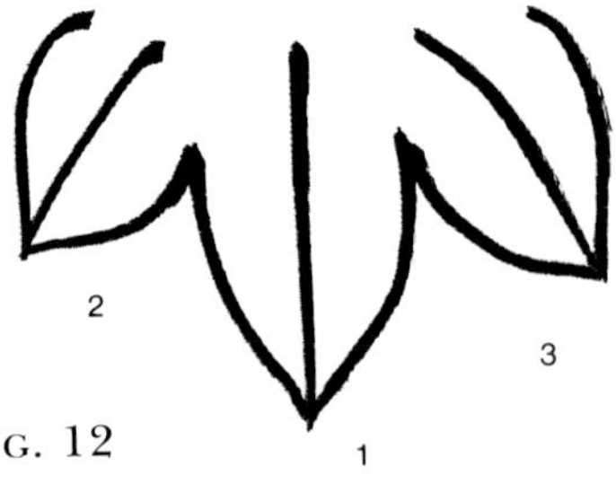

2

3

1

FIG. 12

FIG. 13 For the older leaves add sap green to the outer three-quarters of the leaf and add indigo at the base. Blend from the indigo out. Paint over the centre vein—this will later be reinforced in colour.

For the younger leaves place sap green at the base of the leaf and red on the tip. Blend from the red down over the green. When the colours are dry add the veins: indigo for the older leaves, and red for the younger.

FIGS. 14a, b, c Because of the difficulty in painting two parallel lines, it is easier to first paint the stem in colour in the brush style method of bone strokes, then, when it is dry to add the outline in fine bone strokes of dark black. Add the left and top lines first then the right and bottom ones to maintain an even width of stem (reverse these last two steps for left-handed painters).

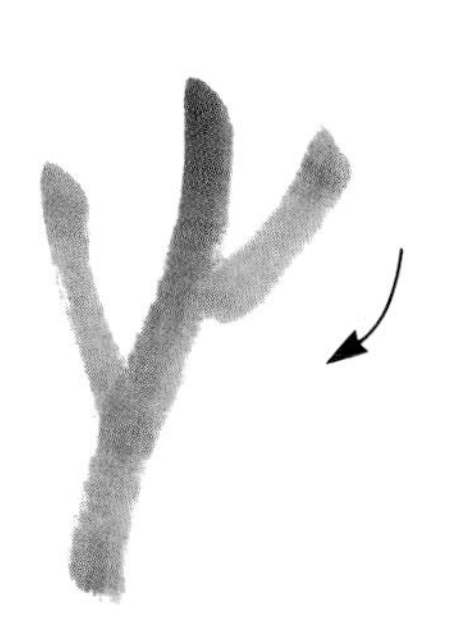

FIG. 14a

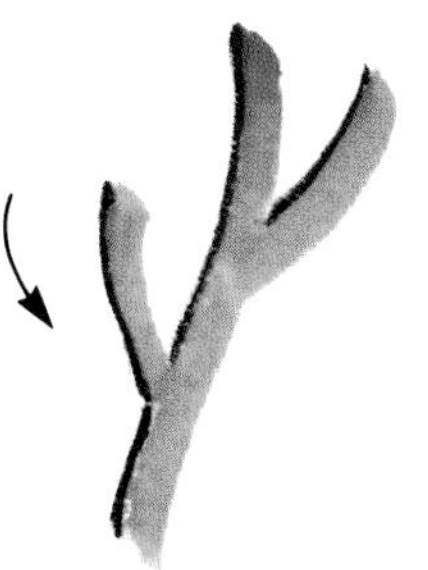

FIG. 14b

FIG. 14c

Fig. 15 In the finished composition paint all of the outlines before applying all of the colours in the same order as the outlines, then add the details. This is the same order of procedure as in the outlined rose described at the start of Chapter 12.

Outline

Start with the flowers and bud then the leaves, calyx and stem (this in brush strokes) then add the young leaves off the stem. These leaves are outlined by doing the centre vein first then each side in one jagged line, then the stem outlines. Finally add the butterfly.

Colour

The calyx is in sap green blended with indigo. The small leaves are in sap green blended with red. The butterfly's body is in sap green blended with burnt sienna at the top of each body segment. The wings are a light blue blended with purple at their base and the wing outline and markings are in a reddish purple as are the eyes and antennae. This butterfly is described in Chapter 11 Fig. 9 (p. 58).

BIRD AND HIBISCUS

Fig. 16 This involved composition can be divided into three interrelated parts, the bird which is the host, the hibiscus which is the guest and the branch, which the bird sits upon, is the servant. They are painted one at a time in this order thus simplifying the composition. All the outlines are done first.

Bird

As described in Chapter 18 Fig. 8a (p. 121). The differences in the colouring are because white is placed around the face and an undercoat of white is applied to the underside of the bird before a pale orange is applied on the breast and yellow near the tail, with most of the underside staying white. These two colours are blended towards each other over the white. Add a small amount of white to the yellow of the tuft and blend it with brown near the beak. There is no undercoat of white here. Some white is added to the indigo and burnt sienna to produce the grey of the

Fig. 15

Fig. 16

beak. This use of white prevents the colours from sinking into the brown silk and appearing dull, which would not be suitable for the vitality of the bird. The light blue should be all right as it is but mix it with some white if required. The grey outline may need to be reinforced after the colour has been added, and the black outline of the beak may require to be strengthened.

Flowers

The flowers and the buds are first given a layer of white all over then when it is dry a second coat of white is applied to the outer areas of each petal, about three-quarters of the way towards the centre. The central area is coloured in rose madder and blended out over the white leaving the top third edge of the petal in pure white.

Leaves

Each is in a number of narrow segments. Outline the central segment first, working back to the rear segments. No centre veins are added at this stage. The older leaves, of five segments, are in sap green and indigo. The younger leaves, of three segments, are in sap green and red. The calyx is in sap green and indigo.

After adding the colours don't forget to outline the stem and reinforce the other outlines where necessary. Add one central vein to each segment of each leaf, using sap green mixed with yellow and white for the older leaves, and adding red to this mixture for the veins of the young leaves. Now complete the flowers. These are given a lot of detail to enhance their beauty and bring attention to them so that they are not dominated by the bird. Use a watercolour gold paint for the outlines: acrylic gold can also be used but these tend to be a little thick and need to be diluted (gold ink is usually too diluted to give enough strength of colour). Add the veins in rose madder mixed with white. The pistils are in red mixed with purple. Add white for the pollen dots and overlay them with yellow.

Branch

This supports the bird and is added in brush style so as not to draw the eye away from the other elements. It remains efficient and unobtrusive, like a traditional Chinese servant. Use burnt sienna tipped in black for the branch. Begin on the left edge of the composition and paint towards the tip of the branch, making sure that the bird is firmly attached to the branch. The leaves on this branch are in sap green tipped in red and are painted as for the very small leaves on the hydrangea Chapter 9 Fig. 7 (p. 46), in single strokes from their tips to the branch. The veins are in the same colour as the veins on the young leaves of the hibiscus. Add moss dots on the branch in indigo mixed with black.

SILK PRINTING PRINCIPLES

Before beginning a silk painting here are some helpful principles to ensure good results.

Always use light grey for the outline of flower petals. This indicates a soft, fragile aspect and, as a coloured line is usually added to increase the beauty of the petals, if the first line is light the coloured line will not be dulled by it.

Use dark outlines for leaves, stems and branches. This indicates strength and resilience. The outline must be dark enough to remain strong after the colour wash has been added. If the colour should bleed over the line simply form an extra leaf. Special care must be taken in colouring the head of the bird as it is best to keep this area clear.

When applying colour the technique is quite different from on rice paper. Place the lighter colour on the area required before placing the darker colour next to it. Blend the edge of the darker colour into the lighter colour—not the other way around—as the darker colour will be the wetter and thus the easiest to blend. Also, it is easier for the dark colour to influence the lighter and produce a natural gradation of tone. Do not colour in too many areas at once, to avoid the difficulty of blending dried areas.

To maintain speed and ease of working, it is best to use three brushes, one for the light colour, one for the darker colour—both white-haired brushes—and one old stiffer red-haired brush with just a small amount of clean water for blending the two colours. Make sure the blending is smooth and gradual. The blending brush may need to be washed occasionally.

A fine, pointed brush will be needed for the outlining and veining. Old brushes are quite suitable for the colouring especially as the silk tends to be abrasive and wear the brushes out quicker than rice paper does.

Make sure each outlined section has at least two colours blended on it to avoid lifeless flat areas. When all the colouring has been completed check that no outline area and no veins have been missed. As each section is blended any spaces that were left can be filled in with the tip of the appropriate brush.

Silk when sized will not bleed as readily as rice paper, but it will still soak up a lot of paint (it tends to absorb down into the fabric instead of across the surface as rice paper does). It is quite acceptable to turn the silk around for ease of working when doing the outline or the colouring. If after adding the colour the black outlines are found to be too light they can be redone though this is double-outlining, a variation of style. Use the strip of silk that has been folded over on the back as a testing area for consistency of paint, strength of tone etc.

Take care to protect the surface of the silk as it is easy to scratch: even a fingernail can leave a mark. This is the slowest method of Chinese painting. Fig. 15 will take about two hours to do and Fig. 16 three to four hours, as compared with a brush style painting of either, which would take about half an hour. The brush style method relies on spontaneity and therefore must be completed at the one sitting so that the creative moment is not lost. The **outline** style can be left at various stages for later completion, especially between the three distinctive stages of black outline (host), colour wash (guest) and final details (servant). For continuity of colour it is best to complete all areas of the same colour at the one sitting.

鳥

CHAPTER 18

BIRDS

Small birds are a graceful complement to a branch of bright flowers; they add vigour in their activeness and humour in their antics. They are the bright jewels that sparkle amid a green dress of leaves giving added brilliance and wealth to the whole. Practise them often, to polish them so that they shine and become the focal point of the composition. Large birds—storks, eagles etc—are included in the category of animals.

The bird is the host to the guest of the flowers.

Basic proportions for small birds are: the body is approximately twice as long as the head, and the tail is shorter than the body but longer than the head. In Fig. 2 the head, body and tail are all in the same line. For a more active posture, as in Figs. 8b or 8c, the head, body and tail are at sharp angles to each other to suggest a sudden change of movement. For the outline use a fine red-haired brush loaded with wet, dark black. The birds are painted from the beak and eye, top of head, back of wings, to the tail and the underside.

FIG. 1 Begin with two short strokes for the top of the beak. Add the underside of the beak in slightly shorter strokes to form an overbite. Add a circle for the eye with an eye dot inside, leaving a small bit of white to add a gleam.

Fig. 2 Use curved bone strokes to construct the head then the body and tail, each stroke moving in the direction shown. Use light grey and an orchid leaf stroke to paint the soft underside of the head and body, beginning with the beak, in a series of short strokes for ruffled feathers. Add the legs out from the body with bone strokes in dark black, keeping them well to the base of the body from which they grow.

Fig. 3 Apply the colour wash with a white haired brush. Use yellow tipped in burnt sienna for the head: begin behind the beak and go to the back of the head, then under the neck. Re-tip the brush in burnt sienna for the body and again for the tail. Use yellow tipped in purple for the underside, from the neck to the end of the tail leaving a white collar around the neck.

Fig. 4 Add the wing and tail markings when the wash is dry. Use vigorous strokes with dark black, each stroke moving from top to bottom. Add the branch at right angles to the line of the body, not parallel with it as this would be too static. This bird is used in Chapter 19 Fig. 3 (p. 127).

Fig. 5 A bird three-quarters face on. Less of the back is seen and more of the underside. When painting the initial outline, leave a gap above the bottom of the wing and tail to later add the branch before adding the colour to the bird. The later addition of colour and wing markings will produce continuity between the top and bottom sections. Use light blue tipped in indigo for the head, body and tail. Use water tipped in burnt sienna for the underneath shading. Use yellow for the beak and around the eye. The branch is in burnt sienna tipped in indigo.

Fig. 6a For the white bird used in Chapter 16 Fig. 3 (p. 101) begin with the beak and eye as for the previous bird's then with a light grey on the brush draw the basic outline from the back of the head to the back of the wing and tail then the underside, painting each line top to bottom. On coloured paper this outline is then filled in with one or two coats of white.

Fig. 6b When the coats of white are dry, or on white paper directly after the grey outline, reinforce the outline and add the wing, tail and face markings using light blue toned with indigo with fine bone or hook strokes as appropriate, as in Chapter 17 Fig. 6 (p. 106) and Fig. 4 (p. 105). Add a pale blue wash to the inside edge of the wing, tail and face markings: blend these into the paper or the white paint. Add pale red feet and yellow for the beak and eye. Add the claws with short needle strokes in black as for the thorns on the rose.

FIG. 7 A turned head produces movement—something has caught the bird's attention—more is implied than is stated, a very important precept of Chinese painting.

After the outline add the yellow-green on the lower half of the back of the body. With the brush loaded with sap green and tipped in indigo, begin on the head behind the beak and colour down the head and the top half of the body. Finish with individual strokes that overlap and blend into the yellow-green area, which should still be damp. Use a brush loaded with a small amount of water and tipped in rose madder for the underside of the body. Paint the feet in red toned with black. Finally add the black wing and tail markings. This bird is used in Chapter 13 Fig. 8a (p. 76).

DIFFERENT POSTURES

Fig. 8a A back view. Use a light blue tipped in indigo for the face markings and the wings and tail. Use yellow tipped with a bit of sap green for the tuft on the top of the head, and yellow tipped with purple for the underside of the body. Use light blue toned with black for the grey of the beak. Add the wing markings in sharp strokes. Add a brush style branch in burnt sienna tipped in black. This bird is used in Chapter 17 Fig. 16 (p. 112).

Fig. 8b A front view. The head and body colour is lightly tipped with indigo. The tuft and underside of the body and tail are in yellow tipped with burnt sienna. Use burnt sienna mixed with indigo for the markings on the underside of the body and tail. Paint the whole bird before adding a brush style branch across the body using burnt sienna tipped in black. There is no need to leave a gap for the branch as in Fig. 5 as the branch is dark enough to cover the body. This bird is used in Chapter 20 Fig. 1 (p. 139).

Fig. 8a

Fig. 8b

Fig. 8c A downward looking posture. After painting the beak and the eye, paint the round line for the top of the head before adding the body and the tail. There are two separate areas underneath. Keep the body lines at a sharp angle to the head for the correct posture. Use sap green mixed with yellow and tipped in indigo for the head, body and tail. Use water tipped in yellow then a bit of red for the underneath. This bird is used in two postures in Chapter 19 Fig. 6 (p. 133).

CHAPTER 19

MORE COMPOSITIONS

The style of outline painting reflects the quality of 'refined elegance' where harmony is expressed through order and clarity. The mood of the paintings in this chapter reflect the quality of 'rhythmic vitality' where harmony is expressed by its dynamic aspects of vigorous abundance. Sometimes the composition includes a bird or butterfly in the refined outline method. This provides a moment of calm and heightens the simplicity of the brush strokes by the complementary balance of opposites.

All the paintings in this chapter were originally 20 by 30 cm, a comfortable size to work. Some of the paintings include a seal to show their balanced placement in a composition. The characters read Nay-Lee, my painting name.

Flowers are painted slowly and gently for a fragile quality. Leaves are painted quickly with a variety of tone for an abundant flexible quality. Stems are painted confidently and precisely for a strong quality. Branches are painted rapidly and boldly for a rugged aspect. Veins are painted with controlled vitality for sustaining the structure. All this is in keeping with the natural characteristics of each subject.

If the brush strokes are incomplete, if the edges of the strokes are blurred because the brush is too wet, if splashes of paint fall onto the spaces of the composition, then this is all part of the creative moment: allow it to be.

After painting the examples in the chapters on each particular subject, the techniques should be absorbed into the hand. With study from nature the life essence is absorbed into the heart and can be expressed with spontaneous lively movements of the brush, giving freedom to your work, each time producing a unique interpretation that is as a heart-print.

GRAPES

Fig. 1 The techniques for the construction of each of the elements of this composition are described in Chapter 7. Use a piece of backing paper that is wider than the rice paper, as when painting the leaves on the edges there should be no hesitation in going beyond the confines of the paper.

Fruit

Use a well charged brush of alizarin crimson tipped with indigo. The larger stroke used is explained in Chapter 4 Fig. 3 (p. 12).

Branch

This is in burnt sienna tipped in black.

The vine is in sap green mixed with burnt sienna. It is almost *written* in cursive style bone strokes. Add the moss dots and then the leaf veins in their respective colours. The vein strokes are the most exacting in a painting and the quality of a flower painting can be determined by the standard of the brush work in the veins, just as a Chinese landscape painting can be judged by the vigour and placement of the foliage dots.

WHITE LOTUS

Fig. 2 The techniques are described in Chapter 15.

Flowers

Begin with the outline in fine needle strokes using light blue mixed with indigo. Paint the bud then the flower, beginning with its middle front petal. Paint all of the front petals before adding the back ones. Add the light blue wash as for the rose in Chapter 12 Fig. 21 (p. 70).

Leaves

Added in indigo tipped with plenty of black, they are painted with a stroke more like that used for the grape leaves only more elongated and with more sections to the leaves. Refer to Chapter 4 Fig. 4 (p. 12). The starkness of colour in the leaves emphasises the purity of the white flowers.

Stems

In sap green tipped with indigo, make sure that there is a stem for each flower and leaf and that the flower and bud stems continue at the base of the leaves.

Reeds

Added in burnt sienna mixed with sap green and tipped in black. Use a fine needle stroke painted up from the base of the reed. Paint the main stem of the reed first then the side leaves.

Add the flower stamens in purple toned with black and then add the thorns on the stems in black.

FIG. 2

BIRD AND WISTERIA Fig. 3

Bird—(Host)
Paint as described in Chapter 18 Figs. 1–4 (pp. 116–18). After adding the colour wash to the bird paint the other sections of the composition, returning to the bird when the colour wash is dry enough to add the black details. Add the legs of the bird before the vine.
Flowers—(Guest)
These are in a light blue tipped in purple.

Leaves
These are in various greens.

The techniques for painting the wisteria are described in Chapter 10.

HYDRANGEA AND BUTTERFLY Fig. 4

Flowers
The techniques are described in Chapter 9. Each cluster of flowers is painted with the one load of the brush to achieve the soft faded outer petals. Use water then light blue tipped with purple for the bottom cluster. While the foremost central flowers have all four petals showing, the back flowers have only two or three as if they are partly hidden behind.

Leaves
These are in various greens.

Branch
This is in burnt sienna tipped with black.

Add the centres of the flowers with a white dot first then overlay with yellow. The centre dot does not have to be placed for every flower, the edge flowers in particular can be left without centres to help round off the cluster by not drawing attention to the edges. Add the flower stems, grouping them towards the branch, and add the smaller leaves on the tips of the branch in sap green tipped with red.

Butterfly
This is painted as described in Chapter 11 Fig. 8 (p. 57). The soft red on the wings distributes the colour of the flowers.

FIG. 3

Fig. 4

HIBISCUS AND BUTTERFLIES FIG. 5

FLOWERS

Paint them with the same brush strokes and construction as for thos in Chapter 17 Fig. 2 (p.104), except that th colours used are different. Load the brush with water then yellow and tip in rose madder. Paint all the strokes from the centre of the flowers outward to form soft watery edges to the petals. The bud is painted with teardrop strokes.

CALYXES AND STEMS

Added in sap green tipped with indigo, forming firm but undulating lines that intersect with each other and the flowers to form white spaces (eyes).

LEAVES

Begin with a bone storke out from the stem of the flower for stem of each leaf. Use a curved orchid leaf stroke for the bottom edge of the leaf and another similar stroke for the top edge, with one of the two strokes coming to a point for the tip of the leaf. An abundance of sap green and indigo leaves complement the yellow of the flowers.

VEINS

Add the leaf veins in a mixture of white, yellow and sap green; add red to this mixture for the veins of the younger leaves. Complete the flowers with veins in a mixtrue of yellow and rose madder: make sure they are dark enough to stand out.

The pistils are in red mixed with purple, and then the white pollen dots are added (two coats of white will be needed).

BUTTERFLIES

Place them in different postures. They are painted as described in Chapter 11 Figs. 1–5 (pp. 54–6), with the addition of a further outline of light blue mixed with indigo. This colour is also used for the wing veins, antennae, eyes, and body markings.

FIG. 5

BIRDS AND CHERRIES FIG. 6

BIRDS

The lower bird is as described in Chapter 18 Fig. 8c (p. 122). The other bird is a reversed image turned at 90°, that is if the first bird was painted on rice paper then the paper turned over and on its side that would be the position of the other bird (use this procedure to copy the bird if you have difficulty reversing the bird yourself). The line and colour of the underside is the main difference—besides position—between these two birds. The top bird is of yellow tipped with burnt sienna while the bottom bird is of yellow tipped with rose madder.

BRANCH

In a mixture of burnt sienna and indigo tipped with black. First paint the large horizontal, bottom branch from its base working up and out to the tips of the branch then add the branch that the birds sit on, painting it from the lower branch upwards.

LEAVES

Added with the same technique as for the rose leaves in Chapter 12 Fig. 17 (p. 68), except that a bone stroke is painted out from the branch at the start of the first stroke to form the stem of each leaf. The older leaves are in sap green tipped in black and their veins are in a mixture of white and sap green. The young leaves are in sap green tiped with red and are also painted out from the branch. Their veins are in alizarin crimson mixed with a little white for a pale red.

FRUIT

Add the cherries in alizarin crimson tipped in purple, the technique is as for the grapes in Chapter 7. Use sap green mixed with indigo to add a stem to each cherry and add a black dot on the outer edge of each fruit to face it. Add the moss dots in indigo.

Fig. 6

A PROLIFERATION OF PANSIES Fig. 7

Flowers

These are painted with a similar technique as for the poppies in Chapter 8. With the pansy each petal consists of two instead of three lobes, and there are three centre petals then two outer petals, making a total of five petals (rather than the four of the poppy).

Add the flowers in a variety of bright colours: purple tipped in indigo for one flower, alizarin crimson tipped in purple for another, yellow tipped in red for yet another and then the white poppy outlined in a light blue and given a pale blue wahs at the centre of each petal (as for the white rose in Chapter 12 Fig. 21 (p. 70). Two of the flowers show a back view, including the purple one which is painted with a brush loaded with water and tipped in purple. These two flowers are painted along with the rest, but ensure that they are completely dry before painting the calyxes, stems and leaves over them. Add the buds in short teardrop strokes.

Paint the leaves next to allow the flowers to dry before adding the flower centres with an undercoat of white. Use purple mixed with indigo for the centre markings of the purple and red flowers and purple mixed with red in the centre markings of the yellow and white flowers. Add the veins for the buds and the other petals in the appropriate colour for each flower. Give a second coat of white or a coat of sap green mixed with yellow to the appropriate parts of the centres.

Leaves

These are painted in two broad orchid leaf strokes similar to the hibiscus leaves in Fig. 5 of this chapter. Instead of a single curved edge these leaves have an indented edge obtained by wriggling the brush along as each leaf stroke is painted. Fill the centre of the leaves with an additional stroke if necessary and use the tip of the brush to paint the base of the leaves close up to the flowers so that they seem to come from behind them. This will help to lift the flowers up and forward, especially important to help distinguish the white one from the white background. Make a solid mass of leaves at the base of the composition to support the many flowers above. Because of the variety of colours in the flowers the leaves are in only two deep

Fig. 7

variations of greens, sap green and black and sap and indigo. The veins are in black or indigo.

The calyxes are added after the leaves using sap green tipped in indigo. Also use this colour for the stems which are painted from the flower to the leaf group at the bottom of the composition, as for the lotus composition in Fig. 2 of this chapter. Make sure there is a continuation of each stem in the spaces between.

BUTTERFLY

This is as described in Chapter 11 Fig. 7 (p. 57). The yellow and purple touches repeat the flower colours. The purple outline has been widened on the tips of the wings to reflect the purple flowers.

The flowers are the hosts, the butterly is the guest and the leaves are the servants.

Details for painting the composition in the next chapter are given here.

WINTER BIRDS AND PINE FIG 1 Chapter 20 (p. 139)

The composition that ends this book returns to the first subject we began with but with extended techniques, thus the spiral turns, over and beyond itself. This is further seen in the pattern of the pine needles about the birds, embracing and enclosing but also allowing freedom with plenty of space in front of the birds. Thus a painting is more that just a picture; it is a visual expression of the accord that is the foundation of the universe. Its study is a lifetime of absorption.

BIRDS

Painted as described in Chapter 18 Figs 8a and 8b (p. 121), except that they are coloured in warming tones: alizarin crimson tipped in burnt sienna for the heads and backs, burnt sienna mixed with water and tipped in indigo for the underside, indigo for the underneath markings, and with the feet in black. The right hand bird has its head turned to face forward rather than turned over its neck as in Chapter 18 Fig. 8a. To achieve this, just paint the same head as for the other bird (in Fig. 8b) then add the body of the bird in Fig. 8a.

Branch
Add the twisted pine branch in burnt sienna mixed with indigo tipped in black, painting from the left edge of the paper to the tips of the branch.

Leaves
Add two layers of pine needles. Those on the left and in front are in indigo mixed with a little sap green and tipped in black, and those behind and to the right are in a pale mixture of indigo and a little sap green diluted with water.

CHAPTER 20

THE DANCE OF THE BRUSH

Fish swim,

birds sing,

frogs jump.

An artist sings colours to the world. Colours have sounds that are heard through the eyes and resonate in the heart. Light blue is the lapping of gentle waves on the shore of a tropical lagoon; yellow is a high pitched ring of a bell in a distant tower clear through the morning air. Truly a picture is worth many words. Colours blend together to produce a harmonious melody that evokes the beauty of creation.

This is the deeper purpose of art, not merely to produce a picture or to pass the time in a pleasant way or to become technically proficient—all these are commendable attributes—but the strength to sustain and endure the difficulties of patient growth must be drawn from a larger source, thus the artist uses that particular medium and technique to become in tune with the inner qualities of life.

The learning of the traditional technical abilities and symbolism is the start of developing an attitude to nature, it is a language with which to interpret, to transfer the images through the eye and heart to the paper. It is a visual definition of one note strong and clear, accompanied by a soft glow that pervades and penetrates to the essentials.

The use of technique and tradition are doors for entering a timeless world of perception. The subjects are not only visual representations of the beauty of nature but are symbols with

Fig. 1

traditional meanings of emotional and spiritual value. When you go back through the symbol to its traditional meaning there is nothing separating the symbol from the subject or the symbol from the emotional and spiritual experience. In Chinese painting the viewer should be artistically conversant with the language to translate the impact of this experience. The artist takes the viewer's ability into consideration when painting, so the painting always remains readable. The meaning, while stated in the minimum, is never obscure or degenerates into the abstract but is rather impressionistic. Going beyond the extremities returns to the centre. The essence of the subject being portrayed is an eternal spiral, and at the centre is that which is the heart of the universe, as each heart is a reflection of the one heart that is repeated in endless variations.

The particular contains the whole, there is only one and it is all. All of Chinese painting contains this understanding. The following painting is a visual interpretation of this chapter by representing the essential harmony and grace of movement of subject and brush while the emotional and spiritual experience of the act of painting is itself beyond words.

FIG. 1 Described at the end of Chapter 19(pp. 136–7).

Sing the colours to the world,

like a bird in morning song

in the rays of the rising sun

lost in the sheer joy of a new day born.

The painting is the philosophy: just keep painting.

WRITTEN AND PAINTED
AT BAMBOO MOUNTAIN STUDIO
AUTUMN 1990